BOBBY WOMACK

MIDNIGHT MOVER

My Autobiography

BOBBY WOMACK
MIDNIGHT MOVER

THE TRUE STORY OF THE GREATEST
SOUL SINGER IN THE WORLD

Bobby Womack with
Robert Ashton

JOHN BLAKE

Published by John Blake Publishing Ltd,
3, Bramber Court, 2 Bramber Road,
London W14 9PB, England

www.blake.co.uk

First published in hardback in 2006

ISBN 1 84454 148 7

British Library Cataloguing-in-Publication Data:

A catalogue record for this book is available from the British Library.

Design by www.envydesign.co.uk

Printed in Great Britain by Creative Print & Design, Wales

1 3 5 7 9 10 8 6 4 2

Papers used by John Blake Publishing are natural, recyclable products made
from wood grown in sustainable forests. The manufacturing processes
conform to the environmental regulations of the country of origin.

Special thanks to
David Morgan who was the originator of this project.
The late great Tony Secunda (Telegram Sam).
David Thompson.
George Tremlett OBE.
and a very special thanks to Robert Ashton for writing
and finalising the project.

CONTENTS

PROLOGUE
JEALOUS LOVE

My wife was packing a .32 pistol. It was the first thing
I saw. It came around the corner, followed by her.
And she came fast. Yelling. And I mean yelling. 'Bobby, you
son of a bitch. You bastard.' I didn't wait for the rest. She
was mad as hell.

I scrambled into my pants, but all I saw was the black
barrel of that gun – coming closer. Too close. I stumbled,
both my legs caught in the same trouser leg, and tore a rip
in those canary-yellow strides. Damn. I hopped, staggered,
fell, was up again. And then I ran.

It sounded like Barbara was right on my tail. That
screaming was loud, but my heart was pounding louder.
She was seriously pissed. Then I heard her daughter, Linda,
behind. She was screaming too. 'Don't shoot him, don't
shoot.' Barbara's response made me pick up the pace. 'I'm
not gonna shoot the bastard, I'm gonna *kill* him.'

Oh, man, I was like Jesse Owens. Flying. Zip, out the
bedroom, along the landing and down the stairs – in one

leap. I was out the house. I had the drop on her. Then I hit the driveway in my bare feet. The sharp gravel sliced into my skin and I sunk to my knees. Maybe I could make it to the car? It was a long shot, but the only one I'd got.

I ducked into the garage, slammed the wooden door shut and jammed myself against it, hard. I hung on to that handle like my life depended on it. I looked around, over my shoulder, and there was the Merc. All ready to rock'n'roll. The key, the key? Where was the key? On the counter in the kitchen or in the ignition?

Barbara had caught up. Now she was the other side of the door, tugging and twisting at the handle, trying to rattle the thing off its hinges. I gripped that handle real tight. I couldn't get to the car now if I wanted.

'C'mon, you bastard,' she screamed. 'Are you going to open up?'

I didn't have time to answer because she shot me. Barbara put one of those .32 slugs right across my scalp. The bullet ripped through the door and parted my hair just like a barber might, nice and neat. Except this time it was on the right and faster. Much faster. As the bullet whistled past it felt like a bird, its wing gently clipping me, and then it punched a mighty hole in the garage wall opposite. A roar suddenly exploded, filling my ears, and, when there was no room left to fill, the noise leaked into my skull and beat up on my mind.

She had shot me. Oh, man. My wife had shot me. Can you believe it? Did I deserve it? Yeah, maybe. But *shot*? I stared at the splintered hole in the door and put a hand –

I was shaking like a daisy in a hurricane – to my temple. There was a trickle of warm sticky blood, but it was just a graze. Lucky? Yeah, but for how long? There were five more bullets in that cylinder.

My legs turned to jelly. I felt the blood and dropped like a stone on the concrete floor and played dead. The yelling had stopped; it was quiet. Time stopped. I played back the last few minutes in my head. It seemed hours since I'd crept into my stepdaughter's room. Little Linda, just a kid, a teenager. She called me Daddy. I'd got up like I did most nights now me and Barbara were at each other's throat. Supposed to be writing a song, strumming my guitar, but actually in Linda's room. In her bed.

I'm lying there kissing Linda and the light comes on – 'You dirty fucking bastard. What are you doing with my daughter?' It was Barbara. She told me, 'I'm going to kill you. Get the fuck out or I will kill you.' That's when she went to fetch that .32 with the deadly kick, and if someone is about to put a gun to your head you get the hell up and out of there.

So now I was lying in the oil spills on the garage floor. I was scared shitless. I knew I had done something wrong, terribly wrong. I had let this girl run this on me and I had let my dick speak for my conscience, but dick has no conscience.

This was the worst part of my life. I never did it to hurt Barbara and didn't do it to hurt Linda. I just couldn't be everything everyone wanted me to be and still be Bobby Womack. Now, I thought I was going to die.

xi

I pressed my cheek against the cool slab. A drop of blood, maybe sweat, maybe both, eased out from under my hairline and slowly inched down my forehead, dripped on to my nose, slid along a-piece and then fell to mix with the oil and petrol.

The door handle twisted, the door banged open and Barbara stepped into view. I squeezed one eye shut. From the other I could see Barbara, her legs and her right arm, the gun still hanging from the end of it. And it was pointing at me. She looked ready to finish the job. For a moment all I could hear was her breathing: I held my breath. Linda, a pace behind, stepped up to me. 'Oh my God,' she screamed. 'Oh my God. You've killed him.' That shocked Barbara.

'God, I shot him,' I heard her mumble. 'Dear God.' She turned and ran back to the house. Maybe she was going to call an ambulance. I jumped up and started running again, down the drive to the bottom of the hill below the house.

I bumped into cops scoping the neighbourhood for housebreakers and other likely fuck-ups. They got one. I was standing down there in my shorts and nothing else.

'What's going on?' asked one of the cops.

'Man,' I told them, 'my wife just shot me. I should be dead.'

I felt like I might as well be. My friend and mentor Sam Cooke was dead. My wife − Sam's widow − had just tried to kill me and was about to leave me. And Linda, my lover, the girl I was supposedly destined to marry?

She hitched up with my brother and never spoke to her mother again. That was all really fucked up. And it wasn't about to get better.

CHAPTER 1

THE FACTS OF LIFE

I was born in a ghetto. This particular ghetto was in Cleveland, Ohio. The neighbourhood was so ghetto that we didn't bother the rats and they didn't bother us. They walked past and hollered, 'How you doin', man?'

Everybody had to survive. You could hear babies crying all the damn time and I was constantly scalping myself trying to scratch out those damn flies.

My mom and pop had come up from the south. My mother, Naomi Reed, was from Bluefield, West Virginia. My old man came from Charleston. His name was Friendly. My father had seven brothers and eight sisters. On my mother's side there were eight brothers and seven sisters. It was a big family.

My father and his brothers all sang, called themselves the Womack Brothers. It was real gospel stuff. He and his brothers would go to the little church and meet up with my mom and her sisters down there. Well, you know, someone has got to fall in love with all those pretty girls around.

Friendly quit school early, in fact all his brothers did, and around 12 or 13 they all went to work down the coalmines. But they kept up the singing and pretty soon him and Mom were courting. They got married when my mom turned 13 and he was 19.

My father predicted that he would have five sons and they were going to sing and he was going to call them the Womack Brothers, just like the group he had with his brothers. And you know? He was right. Every year my mom had a baby boy until she got to five and she used to cry, 'You can have a girl now.' But it didn't happen.

The first son they had they called Friendly Junior. We called him Jim because that was how Junior sounded when you said it fast: Junior, Jun, Jim. His other nickname was Stony Brooks. Curtis came second. His nickname was The Colonel. I was the third brother. Robert Dwayne they called me, Bobby for short. I came along on 4 March 1944. Star sign: Pisces. My folks had moved up to Cleveland by then – the house in Charleston had burned down – and my old man got himself a job in a steel mill.

I was the sickly one in the family. My mother said I was real weak and every couple of months I came close to checking out. They'd say, 'He's going out.' But I hung on. They called me Nobinee on account of the fact I had a knobbly lump on the back of my head.

After me there was Harry, who was called Goat, though to this day I don't know why. Then Cecil, or Cornflakes, as we called him because his skin peeled right off his hands and to us that looked just like cereal.

2

The house stood on 63rd and Central, right in the heart of the city's ghetto. It was a pokey one-bedroom shack, a small bathroom about the size of a closet and a living room a couple of strides wide.

My mother and father slept in the living room and the five of us slept in the big old bed – three at the top and two at the bottom. I was sucking toes every time the lights went out and tugging at the blankets in winter to get some warmth. The first song I ever wrote was a reminder of being chilled and cramped and pulling at that threadbare army blanket. It was called 'Give That Man Some Cover'.

Getting food on the plate was always a struggle. My mother got relief cheques and she bought powdered milk, powdered butter, powdered eggs, powdered everything. It was never enough.

We used to go out back of the grocery store down the road and pick through the garbage cans. They threw away chitterlings, pigs' tails, nose, ears, ox tails – all that stuff no one else would, or could, eat. The owner found us rooting through the bins once and he couldn't believe anyone would eat that shit.

Chicken was the dish most blacks ate. It was wolfed down with watermelon, only we never got the choice cuts. The real meat would go right to the church. We would get the neck, the gizzard, the butt, the feet with the talons still on them. My mom would fry up those claws real good for dinner.

We had a man come around bringing ice and, if we

3

were lucky, he brought live chickens with him. We would wring their necks in the backyard, pluck the feathers – we put the chicken in hot water and the feathers came out easier – and hang them right on the door.

Harry got sick from all that poultry. He had nightmares from some chicken, its neck half hanging off and still running around our yard. I remember when we started to move up a little in life, I asked a lady once what she was eating. It was chicken breast. I said, 'What? A chicken has a breast?'

Sometimes my father would say, 'We're going to fast today,' and we'd all start praying. That's when I knew there was no food in the house and wouldn't be none too soon either. Sometimes we didn't eat for three days – one for the Father, one for the Son and one for the Holy Ghost – and just drank water. Yeah, we'd scoop up that water and drink down plenty to purify our soul. I was starving, but at the same time I believed I was fasting for God to give us strength as a family

My old man would announce, 'On the seventh day we break bread,' but my mom knew we couldn't go that long a stretch without grub. The lady next door most likely would slip a little something into our kitchen, and that's how it worked. Mostly people all got together, to try to help each other. Someone would get sugar, another flour and someone else maybe a little meat, chicken probably. So we all shared a little bit. But it was barely making it.

We realised that come Christmas time. I was about five or six and wondering how Santa Claus was going to get in the house because we didn't have a chimney. True to form, my father put me straight. He told me right then that there wasn't a Santa and that he had ate the mince pies we put out.

'I'm sick of a white man getting credit,' he said. 'I went out there to break my ass working and get you those damn toys. There ain't no one coming down no damn chimney. You know I practically went out and stole to get you that BB gun.'

I told him there couldn't be a black Santa. He proved me wrong, put on a little outfit and announced, 'I'm Santa Claus.'

We said, 'Yeah, Ghetto Claus.'

He said, 'See, there ain't no Santa. It's just a sneaky white man putting on a red suit that he got from a store in town.'

My mother was upset, she thought he'd ruined Christmas for us. I guess he did.

There wasn't much happening in that neighbourhood. But, when there was, it was always something that would come right back and bite me on the ass. Other boys in the ghetto had nothing to do, there was no TV, and they'd play games: one was to gorilla some drunk. They'd stand on the corner and watch someone get drunk and then beat them up.

One day some kids found a cat that had about nine kittens. They started a fire in a barrel and tossed the kittens in, one by one. I saw these cats jump up, burning up, screaming and clawing at the can and then fall back.

I shouted and cried, trying to get them to stop, but I was too small and they pushed me away.

Then they went for the mother, who had just watched her young get a fire lit under them. Those kids snatched her up and started swinging her around by the tail. When they let go of the cat, she landed right on my back, mad as hell and scratching. I must have run ten blocks with her pawing at me and hissing. I've been scared of cats ever since.

I was only allowed to wander our part of town. No blacks ever went to the east – the white – side of town after dark. The whites would kick their ass. The same thing happened if any white faces were found wandering in our neighbourhood past lights out. There'd be heads butted.

My old man was kind of funny, though. Most blacks passing a white guy on the street in those days would drop their heads and stare at the sidewalk, otherwise they could expect some smartass comment for their sassiness. Something like, 'What you lookin' at, nigger?' But our father taught us different. He said, 'Never look away when you're passing white folk; that's when they will hit you.'

It was nothing to step into a shop or an elevator and hear some little white kid ask, 'Mom, is that a nigger over there?'

I remember when I was about eight and my mom took me to a park. After a couple of minutes a mounted policeman came riding up on his horse and demanded to know what we were doing. I told him we were playing baseball. This cop reached down and slapped me so hard across the head that he knocked me to the grass. My mom ran up crying for him not to hit me again. She said I was too young to know that I shouldn't back chat. And the cop shouted, 'Well, you teach him then.'

From that moment I thought white men were dangerous. It seemed to me that they wanted to stay in control. Blacks were allowed to become athletes or musicians, but they couldn't move out of the neighbourhood. I thought that couldn't go on, stopping all the blacks, all the Mexicans, anybody but the white man from being productive. One day, I thought, he wasn't going to be able to carry it, and when that happened America would not be the greatest country in the world.

It seemed the only time blacks got respect was when they sang, doing something that hurt no one. Singing about Jesus was just about perfect, so that's what we did every Sunday. We'd be down the church all hours. We didn't go to the movies; there was no card playing and no profanity. Just church.

The only one in the family who didn't have truck with that was Grover. Uncle Grover, my dad's brother, was the only one of us Womacks who had a 'night life'. He was six three, sharp as a tack and had us believing he didn't do a day's work, making his money as a chilli pimp. But, he was slaving down on the Chevy production line like the rest of them.

Grover knew how to have fun, though. He always had a new Caddy or some other fancy ride. He drank, smoked and seemed to have three ladies on the go most of the time. Old Grover gave me my first sip of whiskey and he used to sit there and warn me against the church. 'Don't let your daddy take you to all those preachers,' he'd caution. 'They're nothing but pimps. They fuck all the sisters in the church.'

My father didn't go for that. 'Grover,' he said, 'you're trying to take away my kids and lead them to Satan.'

Grover would do a bit of bootlegging and he'd turn up at the house with a suitcase full of green. Later on, he had to leave town. We heard he'd shot some guy, but the police didn't bother with it. I guess they just thought it's another dead nigger.

School was no fun either. I went to Rawlings Junior High and East Tech High and we couldn't afford to ride the bus to school so we had to walk maybe eight miles and it would be freezing cold. Every day. I used to put on a whole bunch of socks to keep warm, but so many socks meant I couldn't fit my shoes on properly.

I would try and outrun that bus, hobbling along with my feet crammed in my shoes, but sometimes I made it into school before the rest of the class. I'd be sitting there waiting for the lesson to start, just so I didn't have to answer why I never rode that damn bus.

Sometimes my mother used to make me lunch. Those sandwiches were special. Some days — no, most days — they'd be nothing but bread and butter. No meat. I'd bite down on a slice and nothing but mustard would come dribbling out. I never let on to the other kids my situation was a little bit worse than they had it. I'd just pretend those mustard sandwiches tasted real good.

I wanted to be the leader of a gang. That was the only thing I saw in my neighbourhood that got respect. When those gangs put on their shirts and walked out, everybody would hit the floor. And I thought, 'That's respect.' My father was a big man, with big arms, but he wouldn't go up against a gang.

So I reckoned I could make it in a gang, or maybe work it like this guy in the neighbourhood called Candy. Everyone in our quarter would get up at six, seven o'clock in the morning to go to the factory. Not Candy. Candy dressed real nice, sharp suits, and he smoked marijuana. He was always fixing his clothes, a real tall good-looking fella.

I couldn't figure it, but he told me that his ladies brought him money. They would all come along, four or five at a time, hand over the cash, bat their eyelashes and purr, 'There you are, Candy.' Candy reasoned he was called Candy because he was sweet. I guess it was as good a reason as any. And a good name for a pimp on the hustle.

Naturally, Pop couldn't stand Candy. He called him a good for nothing. He said, 'You think he is something? Well, he ain't.'

I told him the guy was smart, he doesn't work. I asked Candy one day which of his ladies brought him the most money and he laughed and told me they all did. That pimp had those women right where he wanted them, in competition. And they tried to turn more tricks each week for Candy.

So I thought, 'Man, I'm gonna make my scratch as a street hustling gang member or do it just like Candy with a hot stable of hookers.' And that was it. That was my ambition.

Now, my old man had other ideas. He was an honest, hard-working john and he wasn't going to see his kid end up as some kind of shakedown artist. He wanted the best for me, all of us, but he didn't know what was best: all he knew was he had his five boys. I knew he'd pray to God, 'I got these boys. I told you I wanted them to sing gospel,' but not one of us was showing any interest in gospel or any other kind of singing – or so he thought.

The old man worked in the local steel mill, but he still played guitar and sang, and found himself a gospel qroup. There was Roy, Harold, Joshua and Mr Hampton and they called themselves the Voices of Love. My father was used to running things at home, so naturally he figured he could run that group.

These guys would come over to the house and rehearse every Wednesday night. Harold used to sing real flat, 'cos Harold was always drunk. My father was churchy so he hated booze, but they got on mostly. They used to stand in a circle and sang with their arms locked around each other's shoulders: Harold singing flat, my dad trying to boss them.

Those nights my mother would bake doughnuts, cake and cookies, and she put them out on a big old tray with a big coffee pot for the guys. She'd say to us boys – I was about six – we could have anything they left, but they never left anything, ever. We were always mad about that and began to hate the Voices of Love, scoffing our grub.

When they left, we picked over the few crumbs on the plates and took a couple of sips of cold coffee. Then we'd start mimicking the Voices of Love. We'd each assume one of the characters in the group. Harry always wanted to be Harold, singing flat.

That's how we started out, imitating Dad's group. It was fun, just mucking about. We didn't see it as singing, but we sang in their voices and, if one of Dad's friends had a cough that night or a jigger in his neck, we would copy that too. We had them down to a tee.

We'd nibble at those crumbs, lick the dregs of cold coffee and then go through their routine and I'd complain every time. 'They can't sing, they ate all the cake. And the one with the bad breath, Roy. Oh my God, I don't know how Dad can stand being near him singing.'

One night we were mocking the group as usual and my father caught us out. The window was open and he could hear us joking around and singing like him and his friends. He stood for a while there, watching and listening. We were too busy having fun to notice when he stepped into the room. 'You sassing my friends, boys?'

That was it; we all thought we were in for a thrashing. Instead, the old man asked us how long we'd been singing like that. 'Ever since you started singing with that group, Pop,' I said. 'And Harry sings better than Harold.'

11

My dad wanted to buy us stage outfits right there and then. He was so proud now he'd finally got his singing sons, and from then on we were singing every day. If we didn't, we got to feel the back of his hand. Whack. That was the old man's way; he would give us a clout if we didn't know the song he'd taught us the day before. He was on a mission to scare the songs into us.

Gospel was the thing in the ghetto so it was only natural the songs we kicked off with were gospel, the kind of tunes my dad knew. We wouldn't have known the songs unless he'd belted us around like that. Maybe we would have gone off in different directions.

Dad was so serious. He could never give any one of us a compliment without ruining it. He'd maybe say something nice, but ten minutes later he'd be pressing us to learn four new songs. 'The first one that don't get it will have to strip his clothes off,' he'd threaten. I thought, Man, I don't want to be hanging out naked. So we got to know those songs real fast.

As well as the steel mill, Dad used to cut hair to make ends meet. One day a man came around and asked for a short back and sides, but he didn't have the money for a trim. What he had was a proposition. 'Womack, I need a haircut and the only thing I got to pay for it is a guitar. Is that helpful for you?' The deal was struck that my dad would trim the guy's hair four times and then the guitar was his. That's how the Womack family got its first guitar.

My old man was proud of that guitar. Every night he

came home from busting a gut at the steel mill, slipped off his boots, lit up his pipe and sat on the rocker out on the porch strumming. When it wasn't being pressed into use, the guitar was left propped up against a corner in the living room.

No one was allowed to touch it. No one. Dad called us all in one day and said, 'See this guitar right here? It is very expensive. If I ever catch anybody not just playing it, but touching it, I will whip you into the middle of next week.'

So he left it there in that corner and we left that guitar alone. And then every time Dad came home from work, he would pick it up, polish it down and go out on the porch and play it. We'd be brought out to sing with him. This was every night and we hated it. We were still kids – I was about six or seven now – and wanted to be out in the woods playing, not rehearsing gospel songs.

So one day we were all back there arguing about which of us had got us into this singing. We wished we hadn't mocked the Voices of Love. And then someone picked up that guitar. We tuned into a radio station and started playing along to the songs. We liked Elmore James, John Lee Hooker, BB King, Slim Hawkins back then, but they never got played on the radio then so it was probably some gospel, but at least we weren't singing.

The game we played was whoever had the guitar had to keep up with the song playing, but when they hit a bum note they had to pass the guitar on to the next brother. He would keep it until he missed a note.

It got so I would bust a gut getting back from school

to get hold of that guitar before any of my brothers. I was sick of waiting for them to miss those chords. After a while, I got to keep playing that guitar along to the radio so long Friendly or Cecil would complain I'd heard the song before and try and snatch it out of my hands.

Some nights I would be out on the porch myself, one eye on the fret, the other watching the corner down the street waiting for my old man to turn it. I was left-handed and didn't realise I had the guitar upside down. I'd practise and then, if I saw Dad coming, I'd race in the house and prop that guitar right back in the corner.

The old man would come in from work, pick up the guitar, run a rag over the wooden body and then run a suspicious eye over me. 'Say, has anyone been touching my guitar?' he asked.

I would look innocent: 'No, Dad. I didn't see nobody.'

My mother would laugh. She knew he'd catch me one day and she said she wouldn't be able to save me.

We lived a couple of blocks from the Majestic Hotel where groups like the Dominoes, the Cadillacs and Frankie Lymon and the Teenagers stayed. I would go up there with my father's guitar stuck under my arm, track down the guitar player in the group, knock on his door and ask him to show me a chord. I would walk all the way back home with my hand gripped to the guitar neck in that position, then I'd show my brothers. 'Hey, I got something new, listen to this.'

The guitar playing just came to me so quick. I started listening to a guy called Floyd Cramer. Cramer had begun

THE FACTS OF LIFE

playing by ear too. He had backed some Elvis Presley tracks and put out his own honky tonk tunes. In '58, he had a little dip at the charts with 'Flip, Flop and Bop'. I wanted to play my guitar the way he played his piano. That's how I created my sound through listening to him.

Because I played left-handed – I never reversed the strings or anything – with the guitar upside down and always peeping around the corner to watch for my father, everything I played was unorthodox. It sounded that way, too, but to me it also sounded real good. I played with the spirit, not following any music.

I got good. Then one day I was out playing and, zing! A string broke. Man, I panicked. I was fool enough and young enough to think Dad wouldn't notice if I used the lace out of my shoe to tie around the busted string. I put the guitar back in the corner and counted down the minutes before he got home. My mother asked why I'd stopped playing so quickly. I told her about the string and she shook her head sadly. 'I told you not to play it,' she said. 'You know Friendly, when he comes home the first thing he'll do is go get his guitar.' I knew that all right.

Sure enough, he stepped up on to the porch and said, 'Bobby, fetch me my guitar.' I tried to persuade him to lie down and have a rest, gave him a little neck massage, but he wasn't falling for it. 'Nah, I think I'll play my guitar.' I stalled him, but he got suspicious. 'Hey, you aren't up to any mischief, are you?'

'No, sir.'

'Well, get that guitar for me, then,' he said, pointed me inside the house and settled into the rocker with his pipe.

I fetched it and walked back with the broken instrument real slow. That shoelace looked right out of place. The old man would sometimes fall asleep on that porch, and I hoped it would be the same tonight, but he was sat there wide awake when I brought the guitar back. He cradled it in his arms, started to tune it, turned the tuning pegs and then, twang! Dad looked down to see he had been thumbing a ratty black cotton lace. 'What's this?' he growled. 'Where did this string come from?'

My heart had jumped out of my throat. And by then my brothers caught on what had happened and crowded around to watch the sport. Dad shouted to Mom, 'Who has been playing with my guitar?' He only had to take one look at my shoes.

'Bobby. You come here now. What did I tell you? I said don't touch my guitar. I knew you would be the one.'

Dad sent me off into the backyard to get the longest switch I could find and ready myself for a tanning. My brothers followed me out and watched as I tore at some branches to find a cane. Harry asked if he could have my dinner that night, and for the rest of the week. They knew I was in for a lashing and wouldn't be in any fit state to sit and eat.

When I got back with that switch, my old man'd had a change of heart. 'Can you play this thing?' he asked, holding out the broken guitar. 'If you can play it, I might let it slide. But you got to be real good.'

Man, I played Andre Segovia, Elmore James and BB King. Even with one string short, I played classical music, soul, country and western, and rock'n'roll. I played my ass off. Every lick I knew and then some I didn't. When I finished, Dad was in shock. He couldn't believe how good I had got and realised he'd been real selfish holding on to that guitar for himself. The next morning, he promised to take me down to the store so I could pick out my own guitar. My brothers all chimed in then, saying they played, too. So now my dad had got himself five guitar players.

The old man decided to quit his group and concentrate his energies on us. It was his dream from way back in Charleston to have his singing sons. He'd got that, and now he found they played guitar, too.

Dad borrowed some money from his union and got us all kitted out in uniforms. Rehearsals picked up. We sang in church every Sunday and started touring as the Womack Brothers, just like my old man's group. We'd turn up at religious shows all over and play with groups like the Five Blind Boys, the Caravans and the Pilgrim Travellers.

School took a back seat. We'd get back from a show at ten in the morning, still in our uniforms and dog tired from the night before. We were always late for school and often sleeping in class, and the teachers would cuff us across the head with a ruler to wake us. They were always threatening to talk to the old man about our behaviour, not understanding that he was the problem. I said, 'Dad,

17

we got to be in on time, get into school with the other kids.' But he didn't care where we were at so long as he had his boy group.

My old man struggled to get enough scratch together to buy guitars and amps for us. I was beginning to realise that church of his wasn't looking out for us none. The church was always making collections and the pastor kept fat with those chicken dinners he got served up, and I figured that was OK because they were supposed to be higher people and that was the way it was. The church didn't mind us putting on shows and they would get a nice little cut from all the money when the hat was passed around, but later, when my father went cap in hand to borrow money for a new car or musical equipment, they'd say there was nothing left in the collection box.

Old Grover always had some words to say about what my father was doing, too. He said, 'Your father, he's the same as any churchman, he ain't doing nothing but pimping you. Man, I could take y'all down to the Gold Coast, we could go door to door and you could walk out of there with $100 in your pocket. But your father, he's waiting on Jesus to come and save you.'

Him and the old man would get to fighting over it. Grover also had his uses for us. He'd drag me over to some girl's house to serenade his latest lady friend and get himself inside her bedroom. 'C'mon, Bobby,' he pleaded. 'Just sing a little song to my friend Sarah here and you got yourself an ice cream.'

I'd do my piece and this girl would melt. 'Oh, Grove,

that's so cute. I can't stand you.' And he'd be dragged in there with his pants around his ankles.

When my father got to hear about that, he told Grover that if anyone wanted to hear us sing they could always come down to the church. He warned him off. 'Grover, don't you try and take my kids and lead them to Satan.'

Grover just whistled, scratched his head and said, 'Satan? These boys don't belong in church. The only God I know is in my pocket right here. When these boys get a little older they're going to sing rock'n'roll.'

I started to see my old man in a different light. I didn't think he was an Uncle Tom, but he sure let those church folks use him. If we earned any money, the church would hand him a jar full of coins and that's how he brought it home – like he'd been beggin' or living on handouts – but we'd earned that money by rights. My mother once took that jar full of change and poured it out all across the living-room floor. My old man gave her a whupping like she was a little girl. He then picked up every single nickel.

We could be making $100, maybe $150 a night by the early 1950s. The family got a few little luxuries, like a TV. We also got our first telephone with our own number, Henderson 19708. Man, I thought that was so neat, having a phone.

Then, in 1953, my old man told us he wanted us in good shape because the Soul Stirrers were coming into town.

His idea was to ask the Soul Stirrers if we could open

the show for them. I thought, 'Who the hell are the Soul Stirrers?' I was nine then and I didn't realise that they would change my life around.

CHAPTER 2

A CHANGE IS GONNA COME

Sam Cooke was 22 when I met him. He'd been plying his trade in itty-bitty gospel groups for a while before hooking up with the Soul Stirrers. He'd only been with the group a couple of years when he came into town that day.

What struck me straight off was how good-looking the guy was. He was pretty. Later on, he cut a song called 'Wonderful', and he'd make his entry on stage combing his hair and singing, 'Wonderful, he is so wonderful...'

Sam was about 165 pounds, real slim, about five foot ten, maybe a little more. He looked cool, wore sharp outfits. Always neat. Always. He didn't need a suit to look smart. I wanted to look like him, but in our raggedy duds it wasn't going to happen.

Cooke had replaced a guy called RH Harris. Harris had a beautiful voice, but he was a legendary womaniser, a real lover-man with a baby or pregnant woman in practically every city. He'd turn up in Chicago, Minneapolis, New York City, any city, and be hit for child support, so it became impossible. He wouldn't show up and it began to hurt the group, so Sam stepped in.

Sam had been born 13 years before me, in 1931, down south in Clarksdale, Mississippi. He was the son of a Baptist preacher, but moved up to Chicago when he was a baby.

He joined the Soul Stirrers when he was just 20 after singing around Chicago's southside with groups like The Highway QCs. One of the Soul Stirrers had been rehearsing with the QCs and got to know Sam, so it made sense when RH left. Sam was a whole new breed; he went into a church and did things other gospel singers wouldn't dare do.

To begin with, Sam tried to imitate old RH. That was a mistake, 'cos RH used to yodel, beautiful yodel. You'd think you were in Switzerland. Sam tried it because he thought that's what people expected and wanted, but it wasn't his thing. When he did his own thing that was good too. Different, but good, and audiences liked it so he stuck with it.

Sam finding his own style was a good lesson for us, not just for singing, but also in life: that you needed to find your own path and create your own style – not follow someone else.

Cooke and the Soul Stirrers got on something called the gospel highway. Now this was showbiz, man. Groups would ride up to some sleepy little town and they'd put on a performance, sometimes having church just before. There was a knack to this whole thing because you wanted to hit towns when folks had some green in their pockets. Maybe you'd plan to strike Raleigh or some of those places in North Carolina just after the tobacco harvest. You'd make it your business to know when the auto lines in Detroit filled out those pay cheques.

When Sam Cooke and the Soul Stirrers arrived in our town, he gave us one hell of a boost. By this time, Sam was drawing in a whole new crowd. He'd pretty much had it with the gospel highway thing but there wasn't any alternative. Gospel just didn't cut it with the lifestyle of these guys, who'd be into women and drink. He was a pretty guy and there would be all these girls screaming like at a rock'n'roll show. Every artist and entertainer, they don't chase the women; the women come after them 'cos they say, 'If he is that dominant I want to see what he's like in bed.' They're curious. It's just normal. And if you got a dick and it don't get hard, then something is wrong.

The pastors got uptight about all that, but the church folk had a dilemma: they wanted Sam and these guys to tone it down, but when they looked out those pews were filled with a whole new congregation of kids they could never get to church on sermons alone.

My old man went to see the Soul Stirrers, told them he had us five young boys and asked if we could open up the show. 'They all got uniforms and they all dress alike,' he told them.

One of the guys said we should stick to Sunday school, but Sam wanted us to do it. He told us to get up there and work that house for him and the band.

It was at the Friendship Baptist Church. We got up on

23

stage and Sam came out from the wings and introduced us. There must have been over a thousand people there – it seemed like it anyway – with standing room only. He told them, 'We got a group of brothers, the Womack Brothers. I want you all to give them a nice round of applause. We got to encourage them to sing gospel.'

The kids in town that used to be down on us 'cos we were singing this sanctified religious stuff suddenly tagged us as hip. Usually when we had tried to hit on girls they ignored us, but now we had Sam's blessing and *nothing* came down higher than that.

We had little boxes for us to stand on so we could reach the microphone, which got the people laughing. I noticed Sam was laughing along with them. Cecil was so young he was still sleeping on his mother's lap when we started, but when he heard us singing he twisted and turned and came flying up on stage to stand on one of those fruit crates.

One of the songs we did was 'Jesus Gave Me Water', and one of my brothers cried, 'I gotta go to the bathroom.' Then he started peeing all over the floor. Soaked his clothes. Oh, man, we wanted to be seen as pro, not a bunch of hick kids pissing our pants. We did another song and that was it. Sam was back on stage and instructed the crowd to drop some 'quiet cash' – no nickels or dimes – in my mom's purse when she went around for the collection. We loved Sam right from the off.

His plan was to play every damn church in the town and then head out on the road again. I wanted to follow him, wanted to be just like Sam Cooke.

CHAPTER 3
CALIFORNIA DREAMIN'

Sam was on that gospel highway so we got right on there after him. We started to tour the country opening up for acts, Dad calling us the Womack Brothers. Our harmonies blew people away, although often it was just four of us because Cecil, my youngest brother, wasn't in the picture just then. Kids would come from all around and gather around to watch us and they thought it was very strange, a group of brothers all going to the same school, dressed identical.

We started to get our first taste of life on the road, and I loved it. We travelled around by car. Me and my brothers in the back, my mom and dad up front. We had a U-Haul trailer on the back of the car to pull our gear.

We started touring with a group called the Staple Singers, who had become big on the scene. They were a little older than us, but the girls were pretty. Their parents let them stay in the same bed as us – that's how young we were – although I was starting to take notice of women by then.

The Staples family were very inspiring to me because I could see a different way of life: it wasn't like ours. The Staples drove around in a new Cadillac, which impressed me, and they had their own home where we could hole up between dates.

Roebuck Staples – we called him Pops – was so different from my old man. Pops was always willing to take chances when all I heard from my father was, 'You can't do it like that' or 'Do it this way, that's my way.' I wanted to do it another way.

Pops was also a great guitarist who recorded a lot of great gospel and soul recordings with a spiritual outfit called the Golden Trumpets and the Trumpet Jubilees. By the early 1950s, he rounded up two daughters, Cleotha and Mavis, and his son Pervis to form the Staple Singers. Pops and Mavis shared the lead vocals.

We also ran into other families, the same as ours. Like a group called the Davis Family out of Chicago. There were 13 of them, brothers and sisters, and they were awesome.

We also worked with the Five Blind Boys of Mississippi, led by Archie Brownlee. There was another group on the circuit called the Blind Boys, but that outfit was the Blind Boys of Alabama, out of the Alabama Institute for the Deaf and Blind. Blind since birth, Brownlee started out at the Piney Woods School, near Jackson, at the age of six. Within five years, he was scrambling up a racket with a few other guys: Lloyd Woodard, Joseph Ford and Lawrence Adams. By 1944, the group was on the road, all pro, with Brownlee leading. They were getting noticed, too, and their early-1950s single, 'Our Father', was one of the first gospel tunes to reach the Billboard R&B charts.

When I was about 13, the Blind Boys hit Cleveland and put the word out that they didn't have a guitar player, and that's how I got playing with them. They had a guy lead them out on stage, but that's all the help they needed. It was a big deal for me to get out there and groove alongside them 'cos I learned a lot.

Pretty soon they asked my old man if they could take me to Chicago. Now, he felt sorry for them 'cos they were blind, but those guys were hip. Man, they were fast as anyone with eyes, although I made sure I did the driving.

Brownlee was a cool guy. I used to go up to the hotel room he was staying in and he'd be in there swigging back a bottle of whiskey. He said it kept his voice clear. Then he'd call me over and touch my face and ask if I'd got any taller.

The problem we had then was we often couldn't get served at the roadside diners because of the colour bar. So the Blind Boys would all swing by our house and Mom would fix up a shoebox full with all kinds of sandwiches so we had something to eat on the road.

Archie could demolish huge halls with the bluest version of the Lord's Prayer ever recorded. He would interrupt his songs with a falsetto shriek that conjured up images of witchcraft or bedlam. He started that scream that all the big soul singers that followed used.

Plenty of them screamed but Archie was the first, and maybe the best, too.

That couple of nights I went with them to Chicago turned into about four weeks out on the road. I hung out with the Blind Boys all across Ohio and beyond until the school truant office caught up with my dad and called the cops on my ass. I got dragged back to Cleveland pronto. Of course, my old man threw a fit about that, told Brownlee, 'You were only going to take Bobby to Chicago and then bring him right back.' Man, I'm sure I saw Archie smile at that one.

The record business came calling for the first time in 1954. It wasn't exactly Motown knocking. There was this guy called Sneider, the guy who supplied records to jukeboxes in the bars and clubs in our neighbourhood around Central in Cleveland.

He must have seen our set-up, us with our white shirts and black pants – you couldn't miss us as young gospel kids. Sneider had some kind of contact with a record company and also a recording studio where a whole bunch of groups, including the O'Jays, had laid down tracks. One day he gave the old man a call and they fixed up a meet with some music-biz suits.

These guys came around the house dressed up mighty fine. The only guys who came to the neighbourhood with a suit on were white: the insurance man, the bill collector, someone important, so we thought these guys must have been important too. They wanted to record us, but they told Dad they wanted to record us doing bebop.

My father was not having that. He started yelling that we were true gospel and there was no way we'd sing anything but the Lord's music. One of the guys said he only wanted us to record a couple of tracks and one of those was a little song called 'Buffalo Bill'. My dad still said no. The guy put a few hundred bills on the table and asked if that would help. My dad said OK.

But, it being my old man, there was still a problem. This guy had a whole bunch of seasoned pros ready to roll on the tracks. But Womack Sr, he was pushing to get his own sound on that record. He insisted, 'Sir, if you want this record to come out, I gotta play my guitar on it. No me, no record.'

We did the session. That was my first experience of recording. It felt like the big time. None of us had seen inside a studio before, but it made me feel alive. I felt right at home amongst all the equipment. We cut two tracks and the record company guys counted out the $300 and handed them to dad. We were on our way to riches – so we thought.

The very next day, Sneider called up and told us someone had broken into that studio of his and stolen our tapes. I thought that was the weirdest thing because it wasn't like a new cut by Sam Cooke, just a track by some young greenhorns. Of course, my daddy had the answer. 'I told you,' he told us, still running the line that nothing good came from music that didn't come with a preacher's blessing. 'You work with the devil and see what happens.'

Someone put that record out only with a different group name. We kept hearing those tracks of ours on the radio. 'Man, that's us,' we'd tell each other, 'only the name ain't right.' I guess they thought they got us cheap and didn't have to pay royalties or anything. So right from the off I was ripped off. Nothing changed. The record business started screwing me then and hasn't stopped screwing me since.

Funny thing was, around 30 years later, I opened my mailbox and out popped those tapes we did at Sneider's. There was a note from Sneider with them: he was in the Veteran's Hospital in Cleveland by then. He wrote that he wanted to set the record straight 'cos it was him that had stolen our masters. They'd been no break-in. It was just a scam to get our music cheap. He wrote that he was proud of how me and my brothers had turned out. I called the hospital immediately, but Sneider had died just hours before.

We did earn on the circuit, though, and my father would take all the cash we earned to pay the bills, put food on the table, get new shoes. That was fine, but I thought we weren't getting anyplace fast. I wanted to play rock'n'roll or boogie-woogie.

One day I had it out. I said, 'Daddy, I got something I want to talk to you about.'

He knew what was coming. 'Oh yeah?'

I said, 'Sit down. We want to talk to you.'

He said, 'We or you.'

I said, 'We. We want to change over.'

He said, 'Change over, to what?'

'Boogie-woogie.'

He jumped and started punching me like he was Muhammad Ali. Everywhere from under my feet up to my nuts. He said, 'I'm going to boogie your woogie.'

He knocked me down and I screamed for him not to hit me no more.

He said, 'You still want to play boogie-woogie?'

I guessed not. I said, 'I want to play gospel for Jesus.'

He messed me up pretty good and none of my brothers came to help. They were on the floor laughing and my old man picked me up and threw me down with them.

'You get that out your mind,' he said. 'You ain't going nowhere. I promised God y'all are going to serve him. What you going to do?'

'Serve God,' we chimed.

But it wasn't that simple. Sam Cooke was already doing well with rock'n'roll and he knew it was the key. It was going to enable him to cross over from mostly black audiences to become big in all parts of town, black and white. That was the future, he told us, and we trusted him. Sam explained how it worked. 'Bobby,' he asked, 'you ever been to a white church? You go into a white church, the preacher is preaching. The people just sit there and look, say amen and church is over for the day.'

It was the same for a white funeral. 'You go to a white funeral,' he told me, 'maybe a woman is sobbing a bit, then they go home, just quiet, respectable and everything is back to normal.'

31

But a black funeral, that was different. Sam said, 'Momma is crying, she is trying to get into the casket. People are trying to pull her out. It's like a circus. Then go to a black church and people are shouting all over the place.'

His point was that there were two cultures and they were totally different. 'They look at us and think, "Fucking crazy",' he said. 'We are different so until we bridge that gap they are not going to understand you singing and screaming like James Brown.' Sam's game was to teach the whites to scream and shout. 'Believe me, it's not that they can't,' he claimed. 'It's just that they have never been taught.'

From where us kids were standing, Sam and his rock'n'roll brothers looked like they had life mapped. But the church wouldn't take it lying down. The preachers continued to warn us that any man who switched from serving God to serving the devil with his rock'n'roll tunes had something coming.

We thought they were right. In 1958, Lou Rawls, one of the silkiest singers around and a high-school classmate of Sam's, was in an auto accident. He, his band the Pilgrim Travellers and Sam had been touring the South when the smash happened. The driver had his head cut clean off. Lou was in a coma for five days and it took him months to regain his memory. Sam was lucky. He got thrown out with some glass in his elbow and eye.

I thought, 'That's just the start. Does God punish people like that?' Then I thought, 'That seems more like the devil's work. Why put that on God?'

The Blind Boys were still out on that gospel highway, but the road took its toll on Archie. By the end of the 1950s, he was real sick, and by 1960 he was dead in New Orleans. Pneumonia. He was only 35.

The group got Roscoe Robinson to take over the reins as the main lead. One night Roscoe was staying around our house and grilling us on our ambition. Nothing had really happened for us since Sneider. We were still singing gospel, not rock'n'roll, in those same churches. Still playing to my father's tune, but we wanted to move up. And we had gotten old. Christ, we were *teenagers*.

Roscoe got right on the phone and called Sam Cooke. Sam had quit the Soul Stirrers in 1957 and moved to California to start playing the brand of secular music he had told me about. He had already had a hit with 'You Send Me' in 1957, proving his theory right: 'You Send Me' sold to white folk so he was selling records to blacks and whites, more than a million of them all told.

We all gathered around and listened as Roscoe rapped with Sam. Roscoe told him we were still toiling in the churches, making a little scratch, but not throwing up much dust. Sam had got himself a little house in the Los Feliz part of Los Angeles and just started a new label, SAR.

SAR was named after Sam and his manager JW Alexander: Sam & Alex Records. It had a little green, yellow and white label. They each had a stake in the company and the roster boasted acts like former Soul Stirrer Johnny Taylor, Johnny Morrisette and the Sims

Twins. Sam wanted to stack SAR with acts. He wanted to know if we were available.

We were available for birthdays, weddings and funerals up to this point so we were going to be available for Sam Cooke. The only downside: Sam didn't want to deal with the old man on account of him being religious. He told Roscoe to cue me up on the call. 'Listen, Bobby,' said Sam, 'There ain't no money in gospel any more. We need to step it up to the next level. I want you to write something with crossover appeal – for the whites too.' I told him that it was gospel or nothing as far as Dad was concerned. 'OK, I'll make a deal with you. I'll cut you a gospel record and if it don't hit, then you cut me something I want.'

Man, that was it. We were in with Sam. He told us to get over to United Sound Studios in Detroit. Dad drove us up from Cleveland and called Sam from our motel. He was over in 20 minutes and we told him what we had.

The first songs we gave him were 'Yield Not To Temptation', 'Somebody's Wrong', 'Couldn't Hear Nobody Pray' and 'Somewhere There's A God'.

We picked the first two tracks – 'Somebody's Wrong' on the A side, 'Yield Not To Temptation' on the flip – for our debut single, out in 1961 on SAR, credited to the Womack Brothers, like the group my old man had with his brothers. Man, we were proud. And so was dad.

As Sam predicted, the track did nothing, didn't even fly near the charts, let alone dent them. Sam wasn't going to let that faze him. He said, 'OK, let's keep that track "Couldn't Hear Nobody Pray" and write some new lyrics.'

I wrote a few new words, we ditched the gospel and crooned about love and lust, and out came 'Lookin' For A Love'. JW told us to change our name from the Womack Brothers to The Valentinos and we put the track right out there in March 1962. 'I'm looking for a love, I'm looking for a love/I looked here and there, searching everywhere.' We also re-cut 'Somewhere There's A God' and substituted 'girl' for 'God'.

'Lookin' For A Love' hit big: two million copies big. We were on our way. Friendly and Curtis had already graduated school, but me, Harry and Cecil quit school straight off. Some of our classmates were starting to ask for autographs. Plus, I had a teacher, name of Mr Washington. He always told me I wouldn't amount to jack shit. Yeah, I didn't know who invented the cotton mill, but I knew who invented soul. I reckoned it was Sam. And he had called us, asked us to move out to California. Proving Mr Washington wrong was a powerful motivator.

My father was all for putting us out anyway. He wasn't going to provide shelter for the devil's music. He cut us right off. He didn't want none of the money from our hit and he didn't want us, neither. Some money had begun to roll in, though not exactly royalty payments. In point of fact, I don't believe we ever got paid royalties from SAR. Sam would pay us an advance or slip us some cash for a new suit or something like that, but it wasn't super accounting.

I didn't even look at it that Sam was screwing us. The whole business was about screwing. The way I looked at it was there was a choice: you could be screwed with grease – like with Sam and SAR, who might not have given us all the credit and money we deserved, but looked after us – or get screwed with sand. That was painful.

I never got the credit for the part of 'Lookin' For A Love' that I wrote. It didn't seem to matter at the time. Every time I took breath, a new melody or song came out. I knew there was going to be more hits. I was certain of that.

Sam wired us some cash to buy a car and drive out to California. I didn't even know where it was. Had to look on a map. Sam told us to get a Chevrolet station wagon or something reliable like that. That just didn't rock me. I wanted a Cadillac. I was still thinking like our neighbourhood pimp Candy. I saw one on a lot for six hundred bucks, bought it and pocketed the change for a rainy day in LA.

All us brothers heaped in the car and cousin Henry came along for the ride too. Henry was older than us; he always told us he was our uncle because he wanted to be with my father's brothers, but he was our cousin. He was an itty-bitty guy, but with a great big voice.

My dad didn't want any part of it and he wasn't going near that car, but Henry figured five kids with more than two thou in their pockets would be ripped off before we arrived in Los Angeles.

Sam told us to stick to Route 66. Stay on the 66, he

said, and you'll get to LA in three days. But, man, that Caddy was busted up. It broke down not 30 miles out of Cleveland. We had flat tyres, the headlights went out, there was a hole in the gas tank and then it started to rain. When we turned on the wipers, they went clean across the highway.

A guy came with a big old truck and pulled us about another 100 miles to get us fixed. That ran us another $900 just to get the car back on the road. We took it in turns sleeping in the car because we reckoned motels would either not take us or would cut into our stash. Then somewhere in Arizona we all got real sick because there were fumes coming out the gas tank.

It took us two weeks hard driving to make it to California. When finally we hit LA, that old Caddy wouldn't roll no more and we ended up pushing it down Hollywood Boulevard. We stopped by a payphone and called Sam. He was near scared to death. We were way past due and he thought we'd caught a pile-up on the highway. 'Where the fuck have you guys been?' he was yelling. 'Your old man is going crazy.' Friendly had told Sam all kinds of shit like he'd kidnapped his sons. Dad was threatening to cause all kind of trouble.

Of course, when Sam saw the car he knew right off why we'd taken so long. He put us up in The Dunbar, a hotel down in south Central. All the entertainers used to stay there, three square meals a day. Sam paid up front for a few months and told us to start searching for an apartment. We ended up staying over a year in that fleapit.

'Lookin' For A Love' made The Valentinos hot. People were surprised that it wasn't gospel, that the Womack boys were doing rock'n'roll. We followed that up – in January 1963 – with a couple of Curtis's tunes – 'I'll Make It Alright' with 'Darling Come Back Home' on the flip. I sang lead on 'Darling...'

The next single, 'She's So Good To Me', came out in July the same year. It was backed by 'Baby Lots Of Luck', but we had no luck. It tanked.

By then we had got our own sound. It was a distinctive sound because we played our own instruments, played and sang as a unit. I think they might have given us the wrong name, though. The Valentinos didn't really describe where we were at with the ladies, which was basically nowhere. Rudolf Valentino must have been laughing; there wasn't one lothario amongst us.

In fact, I'd only had one sexual experience. When I was about 12, I had started screwing an older woman. Actually, she was a fair bit older: 32. Married, too, to a guy named Wolf who drove a bus for the city and lived a few blocks away. Her name was Ernestine, or Tina for short. She had a daughter about my age so when I went over to their place Wolf naturally thought I was messing around with his kid.

Tina was the lady who taught me everything about sex. How to give head, how to get head, everything. And I mean everything. Serious. I fell for her, I think I might even have been in love, but I was a 12-year-old kid so what did I know? Definitely had feelings though.

I'd get round there and she had a bath running for me. I'd have a bath and she would give me a rub down and then rub me off. She'd have some nice clothes laid out that she had bought me. Then I'd go to school. Later, I thought, 'What had a woman in her thirties been doing with a punk-ass kid?'

This whole thing pissed my father off, but I ended up sticking with Tina all the way through school and right up to when we left Cleveland to go to California when I was 16. When I told her I was going to join Sam Cooke, she was resigned to the fact that I would never go back. I promised her I would move her out after me once I got myself situated. But I didn't.

We wrote to each other for a bit and I asked if she would leave Wolf. She never did. A few years later – she can't have been 40 – she was dead. That killed me. She was my first love.

We may have struck out with women, but the group was ticking over good. We'd chalked up a couple of hits and I was now a pro musician. That's what I thought, anyhow. I had a black and white guitar the old man had got me, and a little matching amp. I thought I was slicker than slick.

So slick I travelled with the guitar hung over my shoulder, gunslinger style. That's what I saw myself as: a hired guitar. One day, out walking near Vine Street I spied a bunch of musicians – black and white guys – chewing the fat in the shade. Man, they looked cool, dressed in linen, some sporting straw hats. Each musician had his instrument under his arm or cradled in his arm like a baby. Some were polishing the cherry-wood necks on their guitars or carefully wiping the sweat and spittle from their trumpet mouthpieces.

I watched fascinated from across the street. Suddenly my old black suit – shiny in the pants through wear – looked way less than slick against their duds. Where once I was proud of my guitar, now I was embarrassed by the two-bit instrument in its ratty pillowcase.

A guy opened a side door to the building and ushered them in and I hopped across the street to join the back of the queue. No one raised an eyebrow. We were led into a studio, but it was bigger than anything I'd seen or been in before. We trooped into a massive soundproofed room, set out with scores of little wooden chairs and over the back of each seat was draped a sheaf of music scores.

I bagged myself a chair near the other guitar players and tuned up, trying to look like I'd been raised in a recording studio. But I was nervous as hell they'd find out I was just a punk kid trying to cut it in the session world.

I had seen a couple of the sharp session men raise a smile when they eyeballed my broken shoes: they were white, to match my guitar. I didn't look like no pro musician. Then I saw a sign chalked up over by the piano. It said – Session One: Dean Martin. I thought to myself, 'Oh my, this is the big league.'

The guys had set up. Then they wanted to know which part I was going to play.

'Do you want to take the first part or the second part?'

I couldn't read music. The sheets in front of us looked like Chinese. I said, 'Why don't you take the first part, let's see how you play that and maybe I'll take the second.'

We got playing, me following, and it worked OK – for a while. We were cooking, but every time there was a hole in the music I'd fill it. And I'd fill it with whacky-wah-wah blues notes. I didn't figure the holes were there for a reason, I was just bullshitting all the way through.

I made a whole load more fills when the guy in charge called stop. Everyone stopped. This guy, Earl Palmer, said, 'I want you to go through that bit again, the horns sound a little strange and the guitar player with the black suit on...' I looked around and Palmer was pointing at me. 'Yes, you. Can you come over here for a little while?'

There was a chuckle from a couple of the old salts playing trumpet as I unstrapped my guitar and made my way to the front in that tatty suit. I realised I didn't look a bit like any of those pros in the room. It was a long walk all the way to the front.

Earl asked who called me for the session. I played it like a dumb ass and said the same guy that had called everyone else. I could feel those musicians' eyes burning into my neck. Earl pushed me and I finally admitted that I'd just chanced upon the guys in the street outside and joined them. 'I'm trying to get on my feet,' I pleaded.

He told me I had to be in the union if I wanted a call. But he fished out some bucks and told me to pack up my guitar and little practice amp.

The thing about it was I didn't want to take down my

gear in front of the other musicians, but then Palmer called a break and when the other musicians took five for a cigarette I snatched up my guitar, yanked the amp plug out the wall and ran out. As I took off past the session guys huddled in the shade on Vine Street, I could hear the laughter roar after me. I rounded a corner, dumped the guitar and sank to the floor. Man, this musician thing was hard.

Many years later when I was one of the best guitar players around, I found myself on another session with Earl Palmer. During a break in recording, I sidled up and said, 'You remember me?' He screwed up his eyebrows. 'That Dean Martin session,' I reminded him. 'The guy with the white shoes.'

Palmer laughed. He couldn't believe he'd thrown Bobby Womack out of a recording session. 'You're not him, are you?' he asked. 'That scrawny kid with the shiny suit?'

I nodded. 'Oh yeah, that was me.'

CHAPTER 4
ACROSS 110TH STREET

Sam Cooke thought the best way to lick The Valentinos into shape was to put us out on the road to learn our craft. We'd be bottom of the bill, but we had some pretty cool teachers. One of them was James Brown.

Sam knew what he was doing. He told JW Alexander that The Valentinos needed to get hardened up and broke in. They decided Brown was the best man for the job.

It's not like Sam and Brown were close. They respected each other, but I knew Sam thought Brown was an arrogant motherfucker, a real rough ghetto kid. He also believed Brown was going the long way around to getting with the white audiences and Sam reckoned he didn't have that kind of time. He wanted to go straight to the source.

The feeling was mutual. Later, James Brown told us that he was jealous of Sam. Sam was handsome and tall. James Brown wasn't.

Either way, Sam knew that James could do a job on us,

and he and JW booked us with Brown on what became a boot-camp-style musical apprenticeship. Sam's parting shot to us was: 'Don't fuck with James Brown. He will give you boys hell.'

James Brown was more than a decade older than me, born in South Carolina in 1933. His old man pumped gas and he spent most of his early years in his auntie's brothel. After school ended for him, he picked cotton, shined shoes, washed just about everything from dishes to cars. Then he was busted for armed robbery and served some jail time, which is where he met Bobby Byrd.

Byrd played baseball against the prison team, which James played on as pitcher. Brown had hoped to turn pro when he ended his stretch. Later they used this as inspiration for one of their stage routines. All the band wore baseball caps and carried baseball bats. They'd sing and dance, strike one, bop and then go on to another song. You'd think you were watching a baseball game.

Once he finished his jail time, Brown started to work with Byrd, a pianist, in bars and clubs around Georgia. Later, he joined Byrd's gospel group, the Three Swanees, who later became the black music revue the Famous Flames.

In 1956, James Brown took over the Famous Flames. Bobby Byrd was supposed to be James Brown, but James wanted to be number one. James had more razz and was a better singer. He was always loyal to Byrd, but back then he treated him just like a puppet.

Byrd and James were about the same height and they

44

would dance together on stage, but off stage James would twist Byrd anyway he wanted and I saw Byrd cry 'cos of the stuff James Brown did to him.

By the time I met James in '62, he was already a big performer with a couple of hits under his belt, 'Please Please Please' in 1956 and 'Try Me' in '58. In October 1962, Brown was hooked up to play a seven-night stand at the Apollo Theater in New York's Harlem.

The Valentinos were also on the bill, sharing the stage with soul man Solomon Burke, the Texan blues guitar player Freddie King and the comic Pigmeat Markham. Brown played five shows a day and we matched him.

They stuck us in the worst ratbag hotel, the Cecil on 118th Street in Harlem, just a few blocks south of the Apollo on 125th. There used to be a famous jazz club on the ground floor where Thelonius Monk, Count Basie and Duke Ellington had played but when we checked in to the Hotel Cecil – like the rest of Harlem – it was checking out.

The neighbourhood was a trip. There were burned-out cars, burned-out apartments and burned-out people. Hustlers, hookers, boosters, freaks, users, boozers. One hard leg was propped up against the wall of the Cecil. She was dolled up in a platinum wig and must have been about six three in her stilettos, raggedy old tights and ass-skimming skirt. She was white under all that mascara, eyeliner and rouge. Never had a white chick. Besides Tina, I hadn't had anything.

We must have looked like a pack of runts on a day

trip to the big city when we fell out on to the sidewalk in front of her. Five young hicks not long out of short pants. But we were hot to trot and we had money and that's all that whore was interested in. Sam had given us $75 to get us to New York and see us straight for a few days before we started earning from the show. And I was holding it.

Before we checked in, I walked up to the lady and asked her how much. My brothers were behind me pleading with me not to blow the whole $75. They said, 'Bob, let's save it, man, it's for food and stuff. C'mon, man.' But I had only thing on my mind and that was some good white pussy. I told them, 'Man, all my life I need this, trust me, I know what I'm doin'.'

The whore waved me away. She said, 'Damn fool, I got a kid your age.' I could believe it. She must have been the wrong end of her thirties. 'Get out of here.' But I was insistent. 'I don't want to hear that shit. Look, baby, how much is it? You could use this money.'

She asked how much we'd got and the $75 changed her mind.

'That's a different story then. What do you want?'

I said, 'I want it. You know what I am talking about.'

'You're going to give me the whole $75?'

I told her she could earn 50 bucks, but for that she'd have to do all my brothers too. She looked behind me to see a little line of black brothers snaking back across the sidewalk. They'd quietened once there was a prospect of getting laid.

'All these guys?'

'That's right, there's only four of them.'

She wanted the money up front. Now, I was nervous 'cos I'd never done it with a white woman. And this lady was way more experienced than Tina. If my old man knew what we were doing on our first night in New York, he would have killed us. 'OK, Mr Big Mouth,' she said, pointing at me. 'I'll take you first.' But I pushed Cecil forward. 'I wanna go last,' I told her.

We skipped up to her room in the hotel. Cecil went in, came and trotted out within minutes. She'd given him a hand job and said, 'That's done, that's easy.' Harry was up next. He came out smiling. And then Curtis and Friendly Jr gave it their best shot.

Then it was my turn. I stalked in nervously and she had my pants around my ankles in seconds. Whipped it out and we got down to business. It wasn't love making. It wasn't tender, and it didn't take more than a few minutes, but it did the trick. I finished up and the hooker said, 'Nice doing business with you.' For the five of us the whole adventure had lasted probably less than half an hour, but we all felt like we'd become men.

Two days later, we found out we were ill men. Pissing started to hurt. I was in the bathroom trying to take a leak and it hurt like hell. I wasn't going to tell my brothers something wasn't right. Then Cecil piped up. He said, 'Man, I don't know what kind of pussy that white woman had, but it must be dangerous.'

We all laughed at that and I said, 'Why?'

47

He said, 'It's 'cos I'm still coming. I got stuff still coming out my dick.'

Next day I woke up and there was pus all over my shorts. Then we were all groaning, especially when it was time to take a leak.

I thought Solomon Burke might be able to help us. Burke was a father figure backstage. He was a former boy preacher in Philadelphia, but then he'd hit on mixing up soul and R&B. He was some years older than us, so we looked up to him.

Now the thing was, they didn't have no elevator and we were right up there on the top floor of the Hotel Cecil. The bigger the star, the lower the floor number. James Brown was on the first floor. Solomon was just one flight up from him and it seemed like a thousand steps as I hopped gingerly down to his room. I was damn sore.

You could tell Solomon's room because there was always a cooking smell coming from it. As a sideline, Solomon was a one-man chef and vendor. He always had something going on. He made his own popcorn, which he sold himself. And backstage or up in his room he always had a big old stove cooking away with chicken or burgers. He used to carry around saucepans, frying pans, dishes, cups and all kinds of shit, sometimes offering up grub to hungry musicians. 'Hey, man,' he'd tell you. 'You don't have to go to no restaurant to eat, you can have my chicken right here and it's five cents cheaper.'

Sometimes during shows, when another group was on

stage, Solomon would be out there in the stalls drumming up custom for his popcorn or fried chicken.

When it was his turn to take the mic, he'd wipe his hands on his apron, toss that backstage and waltz down the aisle playing his ukulele. He didn't have no band, but he sure as hell knew how to work a house. He could fill the hall with his voice, didn't need no microphones.

I knocked on the door of his hotel room. Solomon answered. About 400 pounds and just five foot eight, he filled that door and stood looking down at me.

'You one of those Valentino fellas?' he asked. 'I seen you around.'

'Yeah, Mr Burke,' I said. 'But this is kind of personal.'

'What is it? You wanna buy some chicken? You want a hamburger? Y'all want something to drink? He waved me in the room and I saw he was cooking up something on a hotplate.

'No, we don't have no money.'

'Maybe I can fix you up with a few sandwiches,' he said. 'Only cost you a couple of bucks.'

'No, that's not what we talking about.'

I told Solomon I had a friend who thought he had caught something. 'He says it's hard to pee.'

'Oh yeah? Bring him down, let me talk to him.'

I told Solomon he was ashamed.

He said, 'Boy, I think you got the clap'.

I said, 'He got the clap?'

'That's what I said.'

I asked him what it was and he said it wasn't too bad.

49

'You notice his eyes jumping?'

'Yeah, they're jumping all right,' I told him.

'Well, that's just the beginning. Soon his dick will swell up about this big [he made a sign with his hands about two feet apart] and in about three days his teeth will fall out.'

Man, I freaked out. 'What can he do?' I asked.

Solomon said, 'Maybe they can save his dick. They will put it on a table and take one of those wooden mallets and hit it – BAM! – real hard so all the pus, all that shit that's inside and gone way back, they got to get it to the front, like a faucet. They'll hit it until that pus runs out of there. Your friend's gonna be in pain for about two weeks.'

I must have turned white. Finally, I 'fessed up to Solomon that there wasn't no friend. It was me with the clap – and all my brothers.

'Am I going to die?' I asked.

Solomon laughed like he'd just won the popcorn concession for the whole of Harlem. 'Fool, I know it's you. And you ain't gonna die, not yet anyhow. You got gonorrhoea and you need an injection.'

I limped back up those stairs and told my brothers that Solomon had pointed us in the direction of a health clinic around the corner. He'd also warned me not to fuck around with hookers again. The old nurse at the clinic didn't care we were Valentinos. She loaded up five big syringes, lined us up against a wall, ordered us to drop our pants and hit us with that clap serum. Boom, boom, boom. That was it with fucking women – for a while at least.

We could hardly walk our dicks were so sore, and we were scared to go to the bathroom 'cos it hurt worse pissing than not. The next night when they called us out on stage, we couldn't dance. We were in agony. In fact, it was so painful all five of us sat on the edge of the stage with our legs dangling over the side. Those tight black Rudolf Valentino pants that Sam had us dressed in didn't help. James Brown said, 'I don't know what's the matter with those boys. They're the laziest-looking bunch of motherfuckers I ever seen in my life.'

James had been playing the Apollo since 1959, so him and his 16-piece band were pretty tight, but that didn't stop James Brown putting the screws on to make sure the whole outfit, including us, was the tightest in R&B. He was on a mission from the day I first met him, a serious mission. He would die for his music.

James wanted everyone to call him Mr Brown. It was like you had to pay your respects to the King of Soul, the Hardest Working Man in Showbusiness. Everyone was scared of Soul Brother Number One because he ruled with an iron hand. His band would play every night in fear.

One time I saw Brown standing with a couple of drumsticks in his hand talking to one of the drummers in his band. He said, 'Last night while I was playing you missed me on the second song, you missed a couple of beats.'

The guy said, 'Mr Brown, I ain't missed no...'

Brown didn't let him finish. He whacked the drummer with the sticks. 'You missed them.' He turned and walked away.

51

If he wasn't whacking the band members, he was fining them for missed dance steps or scuffed shoes. The fine could run from just a few dollars to 50 notes or more.

With us, it was open war. No acts were that friendly, even if you were on the same show. They didn't open up until we got a lot older and they weren't going to take no shit from no kids. It was like gladiators, no one hung out and no one spoke. You had to get your ass out there and do your thing and that was to bring the house down and take the show. It was always a competition: you got to bring ass to get ass.

James Brown made you earn everything. You had to earn his respect to be in his army. Each act would go out on stage smokin', trying to take the audience that night. It was good for us because it made you try and kill the house. I'd kick my shoes off, whip off my shirt, act like I was about to slip out of my pants, anything to get a reaction. Get someone to take note, make them believe, 'There's a bad little nigga.'

Some people were scared to be on stage. They'd be intimidated, but if you couldn't cut it out there you had no place in a James Brown revue or showbusiness. You might as well die. And James would make it so hard for us. He would stand in the wings, watching the show, and when we came off stage he would offer up his criticism. 'That's a piece of shit song,' he'd comment. 'Now the first thing you got to do is strike that song, put this song in here and do that.'

I learned perfection from him. All the guys were

dancing on one string and one man was pulling the string – James Brown. He said, 'You had better not be a knee out because I will be watching.'

And when you weren't on stage James would check you out, make sure you were on time, always neat and clean with shined shoes. He was like a drill sergeant the way he ticked things off – all present and correct. Naturally, when you got into something like that, you thought, 'I want to get out on my own. I can't even fart in this revue.'

For the most part, though, Brown treated us pretty good. And he taught us, too. He tried to teach us some stagecraft because we had none. When we walked out on stage, we didn't take no bows or nothing so he always insisted we should do encores. He'd invite us down to his little dressing room below the Apollo and show us some steps. He was so fast on his feet, he was awesome. Watching him every night from the wings and then learning new steps in his changing room meant we were pretty polished by the end of that week.

We learned the value of money that week too. After blowing most of the $75 on a hooker, we were practically starving after the second day's performance. Harry stole a pound of baloney and a loaf of bread from a store. We were sat around at the Apollo wolfing it down when a guy passed by with a pencil, a piece of paper and a little canvas bag.

This guy said to Solomon, 'It's draw day, you want anything?

Solomon shook his head. 'No, man, I don't want nothing.'

We stopped tearing at the bread for a minute to watch and this guy then asked James, 'Do you need anything?'

'No, I don't need anything,' said the soul man.

We were still in the dark about what draw day was when the guy turned to us. He asked me if we needed anything. I figured if James Brown didn't and Solomon had said no then neither did we. 'No, I don't need nothing,' I told him.

'You sure?' asked this guy. 'Sure you don't want nothing?'

'No is no.'

'OK, have it your way.'

Then we noticed that this guy had his bag open and was passing out cash to some of the other acts and band members. I leaned over and asked one why they were getting paid and we weren't.

'It's draw day,' he told me. 'That means if you're a little short they can see you OK for a few bucks.'

'Oh fuck, man.' I raced after the guy with the pencil and the bag of cash. I said, 'Man, I didn't know about draw day. I thought I didn't need nothing 'cos Solomon and James didn't.'

The guy said, 'Well, James Brown and Solomon got money. Solomon is selling popcorn, candy, chicken and all kinds of shit. He's OK.'

After we finished with James, we headed back to California. Sam was waiting for us when we stepped off the bus. Stepped off, dressed identically and walking straight and in sync like Brown had taught us. Sam pointed and threw his head right back and laughed. 'Oh my,' he chuckled, as we pranced past him, all in a line like the showbiz soldiers Brown had created. 'James got 'em, I can see that. James Brown surely got 'em.'

CHAPTER 5

ALL ALONG THE WATCHTOWER

The next step on the ladder for The Valentinos was when Sam put us out on the Chitlin' Circuit, the name given to the black-only clubs down south during segregation. Chitlin' meant pig intestines. It used to be the kitchen scraps served up to slaves once the plantation owner had gorged on the lean pork loin. It was cooked for hours, simmering on a low heat in a big pot. Man, it stunk up the place.

Before civil rights, we stuck to one side of the railway tracks and the whites stuck to their side. We'd roll up in town in our big bus and set up in a club or sometimes on an impromptu stage, maybe the bed of a farm truck. We'd do our stuff and split before the clan had those crosses burning.

The Chitlin' was real important because none of us was on TV, few of us were getting much radio play and sometimes it was the only way our fans got to see us perform.

However, around this time my older brother Friendly Jr decided he was through with the business. He said, 'I don't want to do it any more. This ain't real.'

He'd got with a girl called Shirley, they married and he didn't want to leave her while we were out on the road. I couldn't understand it. We'd just started to make it, but Friendly knew the life of a musician was a fickle business.

He said, 'Today we got this money, but yesterday we had nothing. Tomorrow could be like today or all our yesterdays.'

Sometime in 1964, The Valentinos were out in Atlanta, Georgia, with Sam, Jackie Wilson, BB King and a guy named Gorgeous George Odell. Gorgeous was some kind of character. He was smooth. And a funny, good-looking guy who made his own outfits and could always lay his hands on a decent set of threads.

Odell had got himself a young guitarist named Jimi Hendrix. I didn't know much about him then, but I knew he'd just had a bust-up with the Isley Brothers and was selling his guitar playing to anyone who wanted it.

Jimi played so God damned loud you couldn't hear no one else. He didn't just play rhythm or lead. At that time, you played the solo and that was it. Jimi would do the solo, play rhythm, play a solo on top of that and a solo around that. It was too much for some of those cats who just wanted a pretty guitar sound in the background.

Hendrix had hooked up with the Isley Brothers in New York after trying his luck with Sam. Jimi had snared an old flame of Sam's called Fayne Pridgon and she had tried to get him a gig when Sam was playing the Apollo. No dice. So he struck out as the Isleys' guitarist.

Jimi had some kind of rep, but it wasn't much. Since quitting the army in '62, he'd been playing around Nashville and the south. He'd got himself a couple of bands, including The King Casuals, with his army buddy and bassist Billy Cox.

Me and Jimi were around the same age. He'd travel with us on the bus and I sat behind him every night. Not that I got much sleep. He had a white Telecaster with him all the while and the only time he put it down was when he had to go to the bathroom.

Hendrix ate, drank – not that he did much of either of those – slept and shit with that goddamn guitar in his hands. There were no little practice amps around then, so Jimi would have the guitar up by his ear practising his chord, bending those strings and hitting them with his plectrum. Ting, ting, chink, ting. That's all I heard all night, every night. And I mean *all night long.*

It was so annoying and I was a guitar player too. I'd get mad and scream, 'Just put that fucking goddamn guitar down for an hour, half an hour? Fifteen minutes, Jimi. Please?' But he never stopped. It just went on, ching, ting, ting.

Jimi told me many times, 'You know, me and you are the only left-handed guitar players. You're worse than me! Your shit is fucked up! Look at your strings, you got the thing upside down.' That was because Jimi flipped his strings over, but I didn't. Just turned the guitar upside down and that was it.

I could tell what he was doing on the guitar, but he had no clue what I was doing. I was making up chords and all of them were unorthodox. I always played that way. It was a big joke with Jimi, who used to tell me, 'Man, you play some beautiful chords.'

I told him about the piano player, Floyd Cramer, who I got my style from. Jimi didn't believe me. He said, 'But he's a piano player.'

I said, 'Yeah, but imagine me hittin' the same notes on the guitar, playin' what you'd hear on a piano. It's different.'

Sometimes me and Jimi used to sit backstage between shows and swap licks. That's how we became friends. I'd listen to him play and he'd listen to me. We were both unique players, but the styles were so different. I was a rhythm guitar player: used the Cadillac of guitars, a big Gibson L-5 hollow body, or sometimes a Gretsch. They were both perfect for what I did. Later, I got into Stratocasters and Telecasters with a Fender Twin amp. My favourite guitar was a 65-year-old Guild acoustic. Still got it. So, when it came around for Jimi to play rhythm, he used to listen to how me and Curtis played and sounded.

No one took Jimi too seriously. In fact, most of us laughed at him. He looked like a beatnik in his raggedly old clothes. He never changed them, wore the same scruffy stuff day in, day out. Everyone on the bus took bets on when he was going to take a bath, but it was never any time soon.

He was so gentle and humble, never got mad. He'd just tune out if there was any freaky shit going on. Musicians would put the bite on him and ask, 'Hey, man, you a beatnik or what?' They couldn't work him out so they wanted to put a label on him.

Jimi always replied the same way: 'A beatnik or hippy. Whatever you want to call me, man.'

Nothing fazed him. Oh, man, you could cuss him out, say any damn thing and he'd just come back at you with: 'You might be right, you might be wrong. But thank you.' That sort of zen shit would make people mad, but he never got mad. People couldn't understand no one getting riled. The whole time out on the road everyone would be freaking about something and there would be Jimi in a haze of smoke in his own world. People would ask, 'What is wrong with him?'

No one ever saw Jimi eat proper neither. The motherfucker would scoff half a sandwich and then squirrel away the other half for the next day. Other times I'd see him munching on a carrot. Maybe he was on a health kick. I guess he had some kind of sense because a lot of times we'd stop at a store and it would have a 'whites only' sign and we sure wished then that we'd got half a sandwich in our pockets.

He had a real quiet way about him. Jimi was an oddball in this gang of soul musicians and he knew it. He said to me, 'Hey, man, I'm not bothering anyone. I'm just trying to make a living, just trying to find my corner. The whites don't want me 'cos they feel I'm imitating them and the blacks don't want me because they say I am a misfit. I'm between a rock and a hard place.'

But he was cool with that and stuck to what he wanted and I respected him for that. Gorgeous George would open up the show. He was a good performer and I know he wanted to make it bad, but he just didn't have the pipes. George was also the MC and he would change his sharp outfits three or four times during a show.

So George would do his thing out front, making the ladies whoop, and behind him you could see Jimi playing guitar – with his teeth. People would shout and holler and George thought it was the women screaming for him.

When George looked back, he would see Jimi playing with his teeth or with his Telecaster behind his neck and it would drive Odell mad. Once they were off stage, he'd bawl Jimi out. George shouted, 'You got one more time to pull that motherfuckin' shit on me, man, this is my stage and when I'm on it this is my motherfuckin' show.'

Jimi would smile to himself and argued that he was only trying to help the show, which would only rile George more. He'd start off again: 'You're trying to steal my show. I don't need no help, I just want you to play rhythm guitar. When I see I'm in trouble, I'll call you and you can eat your fucking guitar, but until then next time I see you eat it I'll push the fucking thing down your throat. If you're hungry, eat something, not the fucking guitar.'

We all used to find a little corner to change before we

went on stage. One night we were all backstage pulling on our stage gear and my brother Harry hid his stash. Put the money he had earned from the tour in one of his shoes. I guess his pants were too tight to carry his roll. It was maybe a couple of hundred dollars, a lot then.

The Valentinos went on and did their bit, but when we came back after the show Harry couldn't find his money. It was gone and Harry went mad. Then he accused Jimi of stealing it. Jimi denied it straight out, but Harry was adamant.

I said, 'Man, did you see Jimi take it?'

Harry said, 'No, but I saw him looking at me.'

'Well, Jimi looks at everybody strange, don't accuse him if you ain't seen him.'

Harry said, 'Man, I ain't got no money. It's all my money gone.'

Out on the road there weren't any managers or financial advisers tipping you to a hot investment. You got paid, then you stashed your money, then you spent it.

No one bothered about banks, the government or paying taxes. If you made money, it was yours, but I always had a little back for a rainy day. When I made some extra cash, I'd buy myself a real good ring or watch. Then, leastways, if we got a gig cancelled and there was nothing to eat I could go down to a pawnshop and hock the ring. I'd pick it up when the tour went back through the town.

That was a thing with black artists: they would maybe have their asses hanging out their pants, but they always

63

wore a ring and a watch. We also kept at the record companies to pay us advances. A little something up front because we knew we'd never get paid royalties or something would go missing. I knew they'd screw me somewhere along the line.

I know artists, black musicians, who don't read or write. They make all this money then make the promoter pay them in one-dollar bills. And they get to counting them. Takes all night, they're still at it at two in the morning so they're late for their gig.

I ain't one to talk because I quit school early, but all I wanted was to read and write and count. If you've got that, you got the ball game. I knew college was some place important and if you went there you had a better chance in life, but my father told me he'd never be able to send me there. He said, 'Since you can sing, that's better than college. As long as you can sing, you can sup with kings and queens.'

That's all right up to a point. I thought all I had to do was read, write and count – be counting a lot of money. Then you start having accountants, attorneys and you set up your business and that business grows to a point where you don't even understand what you built, because now the business ain't just about songs no more. And everyone pulls against you and it can break your spirit.

I was always willing to learn and was never embarrassed to ask, 'What fork do I eat with? We used to have a fork and a spoon, now I'm sitting here with ten forks.' But that's very honest. I would try to live like that, not to do anything to embarrass anybody or embarrass myself. I would always listen to what a guy had to say.

Anyway, when Harry's stash went missing, he maybe hadn't bought that watch or ring. The night after the money was stolen, I woke up on the bus; it must have been late 'cos everyone was asleep. Harry had crept up to Jimi's seat. I knew what he was going to do. And he did it. Harry reached up and got Jimi's guitar down from the luggage rack, turned and threw it right out of one of the windows, and that bus was travelling, it was going flat out. The guitar must have smashed to pieces on that highway.

Man, that broke my heart. I loved my brother, but was also a guitarist and I knew the special relationship Jimi would have had with that guitar. It would have been irreplaceable.

In the morning, it was a sad scene. I woke up to find Jimi rummaging. He was tearing that bus apart trying to find his guitar. He asked me if I'd seen it, but I couldn't look him in the eye. I couldn't look Harry in the eye either.

Jimi knew it was Harry that dumped his axe, but he couldn't prove it. Much like Harry couldn't prove Jimi had stolen from him. For the rest of the tour, they would keep out of each other's way. Harry would glare at Jimi and Jimi glared back. But that was it. George got Jimi another guitar from someplace, and the bus – and us – rolled on to another town.

Years later, Gorgeous George gave me a guitar. He told me it was one of Jimi's first guitars. I could believe that.

The strings were all there, but the neck had been broken off and there were nails bashed through it to hold it together.

I took it to a guy in Los Angeles to get it fixed up. Told him it was Hendrix's guitar, that he'd broke it one time on stage with Gorgeous George and nailed it back together to play the following night. That was what happened on the Chitlin' Circuit. The guy in the guitar shop offered me a fortune for Jimi's old bust-up guitar, but I didn't deal. Still got it, but I threw the nails out.

CHAPTER 6

SOMEBODY SPECIAL

Sam Cooke asked me to join his band after he got back from a trip to Europe in 1962. He wanted to stir things up a bit. Get some youth and a bit of snap in his band.

Our first recording together was 'Twisting The Night Away', which reached nine on the charts the same year. It was also the closest thing to rock'n'roll that Sam had recorded.

We'd make a record, then hit the road to take it to the people live. When it came to touring, Sam was like any one of us – he was after having a high time. He closed up shop, and JW Alexander came along for the ride too. All that was left at his record label was a phone and a secretary to answer it. Sam used to say, 'C'mon, let's get a couple of months off and then we'll cut something new.'

But Sam also had his quiet side. He was a thinker and he loved to read. I always thought that was odd for a rock'n'roller. History was his thing and he read about the

Second World War, Hitler, stuff like that. The more he read, it seemed, the more serious he became.

As soon as we got someplace, Sam would find out where the nearest library was. He pressed me to read too. 'Bobby, you can make things up and write, but if you read about where you come from your style of writing will be better.' But I never was a reader. I'd lose patience too easily. Maybe if I had stuck at it I'd be a better writer.

I was the youngest guy on the road with Sam, just 18. All the other guys were maybe ten years older so I got treated like the kid, by the guys *and* the women they fucked. I could never get any pussy, no time.

The women would take one look at my baby face and say something like they got a boy the same age. 'You got little pubic hairs on your face,' Sam laughed. 'You ain't never going to get laid like that.' Get yourself a moustache, he advised. He also taught me how to fix a martini – and drink one. 'Don't drink too many,' he warned, 'they'll knock you out. And put a cigarette in your mouth.'

So there I was, still a kid but trying hard to look like a man. I'd practise in front of the mirror, taking a drag of the cigarette and sipping my cocktail. Then I'd walk out and see Sam surrounded by women, beautiful women. I'd watch him pull chicks any night, all night.

I didn't matter which women I would try, as soon as I opened my mouth they would ask, 'How old are you?' They weren't going to give up a night of lovemaking with the godfather of soul for five minutes fumbling with the godson.

I always argued, 'What does it matter how old I am?' But it *did* matter and I still couldn't get any.

One time, at a club in Atlantic City, Sam got me in and gave me a pep talk. 'Look, you know how to be cool, smoke a cigarette and act a little bit adult,' he preached.

So I'm sat with this chick and I asked her if she wanted a martini.

'You drink martinis?' Her eyebrows arched upwards. Even in a dark corner of a club, she could see I was just a scared little kid.

'Sure,' I said. 'Been drinking them years.'

So she drank one and I drank one. On the other side of the room, Sam and the band were broke up with laughter at my technique. They took bets whether I'd make it off the barstool and into the bedroom.

She had another drink, I had two. In fact, she set the pace. We had another, then another. The betting in the corner was going against me. Then she asked if I was ready to go. I got up, stood straight and then fell flat on my back.

I'd keeled over before I hit the fourth drink. This lady then picked me up and slung me across her back. Oh man, that really embarrassed me. I begged her to put me down, but she insisted I had to go to bed – and she was going to put me there. She'd turned into my mom.

I pleaded with her to put me down. Sam cleared up on those bets and the band had another good laugh at my expense.

Because everyone else was getting some, apart from

me, I didn't always like hanging with the band. I figured I had earned getting laid. I was on stage same as them when the women would be screaming like crazy. It just didn't happen when I got off.

One thing Sam always preached was to get a prostitute. It was a safer option if you were going to play around, although he rarely acted on it himself. He said it was cheaper in the long run to get yourself with a hooker. You pay for what you get and nine months later you don't have anyone turn up on your doorstep with a screaming kid.

Jackie Wilson had a problem like that one time. He told Sam all about it. A woman in St Louis claimed Jackie had got her pregnant. He had been tipped off that the cops were going to arrest him, embarrass him in front of this audience. 'They are trying to take me to jail,' he said. 'I'm not going to pay, some baby that's not mine.'

Sam told him to calm down. He had a plan. 'Tell you what to do. The cops will probably grab you when you come off stage, but they don't know Jackie Wilson from Sam Cooke – we all look alike to them.'

Jackie wasn't convinced, said his distinctive pompadour would give it away. 'I'm telling you, those guys don't know the difference,' Sam insisted.

So that's what they did, switched around with Sam taking Jackie's place on the bill, singing his songs and wearing his outfits. When he came off, the cops handcuffed him. He asked, 'What are you doing?'

A cop told him, 'You're Jackie Wilson.'

'No, I'm Sam Cooke, Jackie's gone.'

'You're singing Jackie Wilson songs.'

'No law against that. I can sing Jackie Wilson songs if I want to.'

Paternity suits weren't just down to Jackie Wilson either. Sam had a new woman practically every night and it caused more than a few difficulties if Sam hit those towns again on tour. There must have been nearly two dozen children at one time claiming to be Sam Cooke's offspring, and their mothers all tried to make a claim on his estate.

I also got a woman in Philadelphia, who said she had a child of mine. A son called Bobby, naturally. It came about after I had passed through New York in the 1970s. I was there to do a TV show.

At about three in the morning, I made a long-distance call from my hotel suite and this operator came on the line. Told her I wanted to place a call. Told her my name was Bobby Womack. The operator's voice switched from brusque efficiency to highly interested. 'Are you serious?' she purred. '*The* Bobby Womack?'

'Yep.'

'Oh my,' she cooed.

Next thing, she had told me her shift was nearly over and she could catch a train over to my hotel in less than an hour.

She did that and we got into it. I did the TV show, wrapped up the rest of my business in New York and forgot all about it until I played Philadelphia about three years later. About halfway through my act, a little boy ran up on stage, grabbed me around the leg while I sang, looked up and called me Daddy. I didn't know what to do.

After the show, his mother – the phone operator from New York – appeared and said she had been trying to contact me. It didn't seem like the right way of going about it, but I ended up sending her money for about six months. That stopped when I asked for a blood test. She refused. Said it was against her religion.

There was also a woman who claimed she was my daughter. Said her mom and me got it together in high school. I said I hoped it wasn't the fifth grade, because I had quit school by then.

Another time, I was stood backstage and a kid came up to me and said, 'Hey, Dad.' He looked like a mechanic, grease all over his clothes. I didn't want to hurt his feelings so I told him we should talk about it the next day, see if we could sort something out. The next day, he said, 'You remember Fifi?'

Sure I did. 'Fifi, she used to court my brother, Harry.'

'But you had her one time when Harry wasn't around,' he said, 'and that's when she got pregnant.'

Oh, man, they would all try it on and it was so hard to prove otherwise. Anyway, if I did have a child out there that I didn't know about, I would want to do the right thing.

Sam's band always teased me about not getting any action. It made me want to quit. That and the fact they all tried to be my father out on tour. They told me, 'Do this, do that' or else 'It's late, get to bed. You don't want to be watchin' us smoke marijuana, run along to your room.' Sam was probably the only one not into drugs. His wife, Barbara, had asked him why he didn't smoke a joint before singing one of his ballads. She told him he would feel great. Apparently, he tried it, but then couldn't remember the lyrics.

All the teasing got to me. I'd tell the band, 'You ain't my daddy. I'm earning my own money, man. I'll do what I please.'

It wouldn't make a blind bit of difference. I was still the kid in the group. Sam would write cheques each week and give them to JW to pass out and I remember one time I was being riled by the group so I tore my cheque up and threw it on the floor in frustration. I was trying to be accepted as a man in a man's world. The only way I figured I would be accepted as one of the guys was if I started fucking some of the women that came around.

Although Sam's tips to getting pussy didn't pay off, he encouraged my playing. He liked my unorthodox style – the fact that it was so unique, playing upside down and not reading music. He believed that was the way to play guitar, to have a feeling for it. 'Bobby, you know why you play so good? You play with the spirit, you don't play with no music. You motivate me, Bobby,' he'd tell me before leaving to ball some chick while I practised sipping martinis in my room. 'The way you play, it makes me sing.'

And that was it. I would just play and feel everything. If there was an open space I would put something in there. Sam would ask why I had put a certain lick in somewhere. I told him the truth. I didn't know mostly, it just felt right at the time. Because I was a singer too, I would sing Sam's songs to myself and play the guitar so I knew where to make those little fills. I didn't know what made me put a tune there, the spirit just hit me and, whoop, there it was.

Sam had a huge impact on my life. He was like my big brother. He could walk through the door and make anyone feel like they'd known him all their life. At the same time, you had better watch what you said because he was sharp. He told me, 'People don't want to hear about too much pressure, that's why they want us. To entertain them.' People would spend their last dollar to hear Sam Cooke and avoid their life.

He also told me not to get angry at people. 'If you are going to be a star,' he said, 'make the audience feel like a star, too. If you see an ugly woman next to five beautiful women, then pay attention to the ugly one.'

Then, finally one night, at some hotel, someplace, Betty turned up. She must have weighed in at 300 pounds easy. She was fat. A fat schoolteacher. There she was, sat in the hotel lobby waiting to catch sight of Sam because she followed him from one end of the country to the other hoping one night to end up in his bed.

But the shame of it was that wasn't going to happen – ever. Sam could get the pick of any girls and if Betty had been the last woman on earth he still would have swerved her. So Betty had turned to chasing Cliff White, the guitar player. Now, Cliff was a pretty big guy, he could handle Betty, but he could also get the pretty women and had no need for her.

That left me. So this one night I joined her sitting out in the lobby, just the two of us. And Betty said, 'It's hard, ain't it?' No it wasn't, but I let it pass. 'We both got our problems – you're too young, and I'm too fat.'

I thought for a horrible moment that Sam might have put her up to it. It could have been another bit of sport for the boys to laugh at. But, Betty told me, she had had enough of running after Sam and Cliff. She knew they were sleeping with all the hot chicks.

Betty looked pretty down and she was right. If I'd got something else on I wouldn't have been sat out with a woman twice my age and nearly double my size. 'Everyone else is off having a good time, why can't we?' she asked. Then she turned to me, pushed her tits into my face and asked, 'You want some of this?'

'Yeahhh,' I gasped, burying my face in her rack.

We went up to my room, Betty puffing and panting behind on the stairs. I prayed none of the band would spot me sneaking her up there. I didn't want them to think I was desperate, even though I was.

We got started, but it was pretty rough going. Betty was just so big. Man, every time I thought I had it in there, she told me I'd just found a roll of fat. There was just so much flesh it was terrible. I screamed out, 'Oh, baby, I'm getting ready to go.'

75

Betty said, 'No, no, not yet. It's not even inside yet.'

She finally got hold of my pecker and put it in and we started to get something going. And when she came, boy, I've never seen a woman in my life come like that. It was like she had turned on a fire hose. She threw me clean off her and off the bed. It was like she knew she might drown me otherwise.

I was left lying there, between the bed and the wall. I heard her moan and then call down, 'Did I hurt you, Bobby?' I told her it was OK, but I was already trying to plan how I could get Betty out of that room without Sam or the band seeing.

I never told them I had tagged Betty. A while later I found out she'd dropped dead of a heart attack. So she never did get to give Sam any of her loving, but I was glad she gave me hers. She made me feel like a man for once on that tour when everyone else treated me like a kid.

In 1963, we went out on another tour. It was something like 24 states in less than a couple of months. Hard work. And a lot of it was down South where segregation was still the only way of life.

Sam had the Greyhound bus for the musicians and three cars out – a Jaguar sports, a Caddy and station wagon – for himself and the headliners. They were Johnny Thunder, The Crystals, Dionne Warwick and Solomon Burke. Gorgeous George was the MC.

I learned a lot about America on that trip, about race and rights, who had them and, more importantly, who didn't. We didn't. It didn't matter that Sam was a big star; in the South that didn't cut any ice. He was black.

He got busted in Shreveport for disturbing the peace. He'd tried to book himself into a whites-only motel. We'd sit in the car travelling between gigs and his anger would spill out. 'I don't like coming down here and being treated like that. They tell me how good I am, jocks come around, blow up my records and everything, and I have to stay in dumps.'

Despite all the things he had, Sam felt he had not escaped and nor had his people. He lived in a gilded world in LA, a house with a swimming pool, nice white neighbours. All that was wiped clean in Louisiana.

The civil rights revolution was in full swing and the tension on that tour was palpable. 'You know you can't go on the white side of town and do all the whites. And then go on the black side. The whites won't come that side of town.' He always told me that he sang the way white people like. 'There's two sides to me,' he said. 'I sing one side for the whites – "Another Saturday night and I ain't got nobody, I got some money 'cos I just got paid" – and one for the blacks – "If you ever change your mind" – a bit of gospel that the brothers go for.'

You might sometimes have had blacks on one side of the club, whites on the other, but there was no integration, and that's what Sam – we all – wanted. Sometimes the cops brought their dogs out to hound the audience in case they got out of control.

The night President Kennedy was assassinated Sam

played the Apollo and I'm certain he saw a vision, he saw something was getting ready to happen.

At the end of that year, back in LA, Sam called me up. He wanted me to drive over to Los Feliz and meet up at his house. Sam had bought the pad from a guy who worked in sound and there was a fantastic state-of-the-art system installed there.

Sam was standing in the middle of the living room when I arrived. He looked good, he always did. He didn't say much, just cued up a song. We listened, a great booming sound crashing out of these massive movie-studio speakers, and when it ended I had nothing to say. The song, of course, was 'A Change Is Gonna Come'. I didn't know what I could say. I knew what I was thinking, though.

I looked at him and he stared right back – he looked right through me. Sam knew I wouldn't back chat him or talk crazy, but I would voice my opinion. And that's what he wanted right then. An opinion.

'What do you think?' he asked, staring at me hard.

'It sounds like death.' That's what I had been thinking. Yeah, death.

'Death?' Sam hadn't expected that.

'Yeah, it's just so eerie,' I told him. 'It gives me the chills, Sam.'

Sam leaned over and stopped the tape machine. Then, real slow, he turned back to me. Then he said, 'I promise I won't ever release that song.'

It was like he was telling me – writer to writer, brother

to brother – that, if the song was released, that would be it. The end. This was going to be Sam's swansong, then he would be out of there, as if he'd done his work.

He'd obviously just cut it, but it was a total surprise. He told me he'd never written a song so easy. It was obvious what had played out on that tour – the segregation, the violence, all the racial shit – had had a profound effect on him. Sam said, 'It just came to me. Every word was like someone was telling me, "Now say this, now say that. That's it, no doodling." Bobby, this song was like a dream. It came so fast.'

There was a little panic behind his eyes. Because it had come so fast, Sam thought he might have pinched it. He said, 'Bobby, I dreamed this song, man, I wanted to ask, "You didn't hear nothing like this on the radio did you?"'

I'd heard nothing like it, but I knew what he meant. Sometimes you wrote something you thought you wrote, but it turned out to be someone else's tune that maybe you had heard on the radio the day before. But I knew Sam's song was fresh.

I said, 'I ain't heard nothing like that.'

'You sure?'

'That's heavy, those lyrics.'

'That's why that fucker will never come out, Bobby. I'm scared of that song.'

He kept saying that, kept promising it would never be released – 'Not while I'm alive.'

That was one of the heaviest experiences I ever had. The tour earlier in the year had had a profound effect on him. I found out later that Sam had been impressed with Bob Dylan's 'Blowing In The Wind' and wanted to deliver his — the black man's — response. He'd recorded 'A Change Is Gonna Come' in late December '63 at RCA studios with the arranger Rene Hall, but I had no idea at the time.

He used to call me for sessions, but there was no guitar or nothing. I didn't even hear Cliff White on there. You couldn't hear no guitar, just strings. And the death walk thing, that was a drum. That was Earl Palmer. And Sam. Sam was singing his ass off.

We sat down after another listen. Sam was still grim. He told me he had been fighting with RCA and had already threatened trouble with the label if it released the song as a single. But it was bothering him. 'Why do you think I am afraid of this song?' he asked.

'It sounds like death, like somebody died or somebody is going to die.'

'That's what I am afraid of.'

'Death.'

'It ain't the one,' he kept repeating.

But then I tried to take it back. I wanted others to hear the song. It was — it *is* — a beautiful song. But he told me I'd already spoken my bit and that was the truth.

CHAPTER 7

IT'S ALL OVER NOW

One week during 1963, I was back home visiting and I ran into my uncle Wes, my father's baby brother. He was a pretty good singer and had helped The Valentinos work on our act.

Old Wes was having trouble with his wife, Betty Jo. She had been the backbone of the Sanctified and Holiness Church, real religious, a God-fearing woman who went to church every day. Overnight, Betty Jo turned out, running fast and loose, dancing, drinking and partying hard. She went around with her dresses real high and stayed out all night long.

Wes used to wait up for her, waiting for her to come home. He couldn't understand it. He couldn't take it neither. He thought Betty Jo had got herself another man – maybe she had. So every weekend began and ended with a fight. My uncle would scream and holler, 'I knew you was out, out there backsliding and then trying to come back to God.' Then he issued this threat, which just stuck in my mind. He said, 'This is it, I'm leaving you. It's all over now.'

Of course, he didn't and the following week it was the same old story. 'Betty, I'm going to give you one more chance and then I'm leaving you. It's all over now.' He would tell me, 'This is it for Betty Jo, when she comes home tonight I'm packin' her bags and putting her out'.

But he never got that far because she would come in and twist him around her finger. 'Betty Jo, you are a sinful woman, you disrespect everything that God said about a woman,' he'd tell her.

My father would get involved too. They'd get into it with Uncle Wes pouring his heart out to his brother and my dad asking when he was going to leave. Uncle Wes was at his wits' end. 'You don't know how much I love her, well, OK, I used to love her, but it's all over now.'

Betty Jo always had a way with him. She'd take Uncle Wes in the back room, give him some loving and he was happy again for a few hours. My father would warn him, 'Wes, do not go in the room, I don't care what she says. Whatever she do in there, you come out a different person.'

Of course, when Wes came out he'd tell anyone that would listen that Betty Jo was the best wife and that he'd never think of leaving her.

So I thought that was pretty funny – tragic, but fun. By now my brother Friendly had quit The Valentinos so he was back in Cleveland. Had himself a record store. He was quite a little celebrity around town, an ex-Valentino. The name was beginning to pay off.

When I popped into the store one day, I was telling his wife Shirley, my sister-in-law, about Uncle Wes and Betty Jo. We sat there a while tossing lines back and forth and out came 'It's All Over Now'.

People sometimes ask how I wrote that song 'cos I was only a young kid at the time. I hadn't really had any adult life experiences like that, but I didn't need to, I could watch it all play out with Uncle Wes. He gave me the title, the lyrics, I saw it all, man, it was a trip to write.

So the fourth Valentinos' single was 'It's All Over Now'. It came out in August 1964, a real blast of rock and a mile away from our soul or gospel roots. But it didn't hit with the charts. Not our version anyway.

Then Sam Cooke told me that a British group wanted to cover the song. I didn't like the idea but by the time I knew, it was too late. I'd never heard of the Rolling Stones then. Nor had most of the United States, because they'd only been playing a couple of years with one album and three singles to their name, starting with Chuck Berry's 'Come On' in 1963. Early in 1964 they released Buddy Holly's 'Not Fade Away', which may have struck big in Britain but only scraped into the Top 50 in the US charts.

They – and their manager Andrew Loog Oldham – had been working up their rebellious image. They'd pissed in a garage forecourt, big deal. Now they wanted a slice of blue-collar R&B and they went to Sam to get it.

Sam told me that if the Stones covered the song it would be the most important move I could make. Right then I didn't get it. Sam swore blind they were going to be huge. He told me, 'Bobby, they ain't got a whole of talent, the singer can't sing, they play out of key, but there ain't nobody like them.'

I was sceptical, but Sam was persuasive. Man, I don't know what he saw, but he did. He told me not to compare Mick Jagger with how we sung. Or how he sung. Sam and Mick were like chalk and cheese as singers and performers and I thought I knew who was cheese. But, Sam said, they're stylish, nobody sounds like Mick or the band. 'You can't get that at the drugstore,' he told me. 'You can only get it from Mick. That's what makes him pretty powerful.'

A lot more songwriters like me had begun to sing their own songs rather than hand them to a band to perform. The writer knew the song backwards, they'd lived it, knew what the song was about. Mick Jagger and Keith Richards hadn't started writing their own tunes by then. They were still relying on guys like me, Chuck Berry and Howlin' Wolf, who gave them 'Little Red Rooster'.

I made a stink about them recording the song. I would tell anyone that would listen that the Rolling Stones could go fuck themselves. 'Fuckers, why wait for me to create something? Why don't they get their own song?' I'd ask. 'Every time, the white boys come and steal from the brothers and take their music.'

They'd done it anyway. At Chess in Chicago, and it came out on the *12x5* LP. And then 'It's All Over Now' became their first UK No 1. I was still screaming and hollering right up until I got my first royalty cheque from the song. Man, the amount of money rolling in shut me right up. I have been chasing the Stones ever since trying to get them to record another of my songs.

I got a call early in December 1964. Sam asked me up to his house again. It was a Thursday, around lunchtime. 'I got to talk to you about something very important. I've made some decisions.'

I'd been over many times since he played 'A Change Is Gonna Come' to me. Sam had still kept the record under wraps, but I knew from the tone of his voice something was up. I didn't know what, but I thought up a whole lot of stuff and more on that ride over there. None of it prepared me for what I heard.

I got there. We had a drink. I knew Sam had something weighing on his mind. I didn't have to wait long to find out what it was.

He told me, 'The label is hitting me for money, you guys need some money. I'm killing myself trying to run the whole company. I'm payin' out, payin' out, payin' out.'

He told me he couldn't make any serious money out on the road, that had run its course; don't forget he had a lot of people on some of those bills. Then there was the band to pay.

'I spend more money than I make doing one-nighters,' he explained.

Then he laid it out. He'd been talking to Sammy Davis Jr Sammy wanted Sam in Vegas, and Sam was keen. He knew Sammy knew Vegas inside out. Sam was going to play all the big lounges.

That was the first bombshell. The next went like this: 'Bobby, I'm getting rid of you as my guitarist.' It hit me like a body blow. I could hear Sam talking, but I wasn't listening. It was just noise. 'Getting rid of you...'

Getting rid of me? The plan was just to keep Cliff on. Sam kept at it: 'Your group, your brothers have suffered tremendously with me being selfish and having you on the road playing guitar for me,' he explained.

I didn't agree, but my throat was dry. I didn't say a thing.

He told me I was the lead singer of The Valentinos, the guitarist and songwriter. 'I'm going to put into your career because you could all be as big as The Beatles.' He thought we could be out there making hits and opening up new markets, talking like a record-company man.

I was still reeling from being dropped as his guitarist. He must have seen it and tried to soften the blow. 'Not that I don't want you to play with me,' he said. 'It's a tough decision to make. Much as I like to hear you playing with me I can't help but see your brothers sitting over there at the apartment waiting on you to come home.'

I knew that. When I came off the road with Sam, I would go back to the apartment with food and other junk I'd collected on the road. My brothers would wait for me to put it on the table – like a peace offering.

He said, 'Don't leave your brothers, you could be huge. Being brothers is very unique.'

While I let that sink in, Sam laid out his idea for The Valentinos to become the next big black group.

'I'm going to set up some dates for you guys because I can't just keep going into my pocket and just keep giving everyone from the company money while we wait on a record,' he said. 'I want you to go out and make some money.'

This was a big surprise. I still couldn't get my head around it. I checked, 'I ain't going to be playing with you no more?'

'No, man, you're going to sing, write and go forward.'

It was like he'd knocked me down. I enjoyed being around Sam, learning from him as a writer. And a man. Now, I was on my own again. Or, at least, with my brothers. There didn't seem much more to be said. I got up to leave. Then, for the first time, I noticed what Sam was wearing. He was dressed in a pair of pyjamas. Checked pyjamas. Those were the last clothes I ever saw him in.

A week or so after my drive up to Sam's house, The Valentinos left to go on the road. First stop Houston, Texas. I'll never forget it. We checked into a motel, checked into bed and fell fast asleep. Halfway through the night someone started knocking on all the doors. Then I heard a lot of shouting. Some guy was going down the corridor. Then I got a knock and the guy on the other side of the door simply said, 'Sam's dead,' and banged on the next room's door. I was half-asleep. I couldn't take it in. I heard it again, 'Sam Cooke is dead.' The man was my mentor, a second father. Dead.

87

I turned on the news and there it was on every bulletin. Sam Cooke was dead. Man, that was it. The tour was dead. We got right back in the bus, turned it around and headed for LA.

There were all sorts of stories about Sam's death in the weeks, months and years that followed. That he'd been hit by the mafia. That the white establishment or record business wanted him dead. There were so many conflicting versions of the events of that night, too, but the simple truth was that it was a tragic end and a terrible waste of a life.

The official report ran something like this:

At around 9pm on 10 December 1964, Sam met record producer Al Schmitt and his wife, Joan for dinner at Martoni's, an LA restaurant. The threesome had a couple of martinis. They were joined in a booth by Elisa Boyer, a 22-year-old. Later that night Sam left Martoni's with Boyer, but arranged to meet the Schmitts at the Sunset Boulevard nightspot PJs at around 1am.

They only stuck around for a short time, then took the freeway south and arrived at the Hacienda Motel, a $3-a-room joint at 9131 Figueroa Street in Watts. They checked in at 2.35am. Cooke signed in under his own name.

The pair took a room. A few minutes later Boyer, dressed only in her underwear and carrying hers and Cooke's clothing, knocked on the door of motel manager Bertha Franklin. Franklin was on the phone to the motel's owner, Evelyn Carr. When she heard the knocking she went to investigate, but Boyer was impatient and had already fled.

Franklin returned to the phone. A few moments later she was disturbed by more knocking. Franklin again broke off her conversation with Carr. This time it was Cooke banging on the door, dressed only in an overcoat and shoes. He asked where Boyer had gone. Franklin told him she had no idea. He left. Cooke got in his car and pulled off, but then had a change of plan.

He returned to the motel reception and asked to search Franklin's apartment for Boyer. Franklin refused. Cooke broke the door down and there was a fight. Franklin reached for a .22 handgun she kept on her TV set and shot three times at close range. Two bullets missed Cooke, a third penetrated his heart and lungs.

The police were called twice at around 3am – once by Boyer from a payphone a couple of blocks from the Hacienda and also by Carr. Carr, who had listened in on the open phone line while Sam and Franklin fought, was a witness. She told police, 'A guy just broke the door. I think she shot him.'

The way I saw it, Sam was a womaniser. No question. We would party and JW would tell Sam to go home. Sam would get a dozen raw eggs, beat them up real good and drink them. Or oysters. I said, 'You think that will work?'

He said, 'Yeah, man, I gotta fuck when I get home, man, or my wife will know.'

When I asked Barbara about it later, she said Sam

couldn't raise a match when he got home. It could have been that with Boyer, the broad he picked up, he thought, 'I'm fucking her tonight. I'm going to knock this broad off.'

Franklin worked at a little cheap motel. It had been robbed three or four times before and the cops had told her to buy a gun and get a licence. Sam walked in, on her time, to get his pants. Sam had $750 in his pants and $1,500 dollars in the trunk of his car. He was shot in the chest, with a .22. A .22 is a dangerous gun. The bullet doesn't go all the way through, it moves.

Sam died with his arm up trying to protect himself from blows. Franklin had beat him with a broom or a big mop. She broke his arm in about three or four places and she broke his nose. He was trying to get up when he fell against the wall. All Sam was doing was trying to get home. Franklin said, 'I didn't know he was Sam Cooke. He was my favourite artist.' She couldn't understand what Sam Cooke was doing down in the ghetto.

Then, right after, Sam died, man. That's what scared the shit out of me. I was riding along in my car and heard that duh, duh, duh. I knew it was 'A Change Is Gonna Come', the label released it two weeks after Sam was shot. He was dead 11 December, the single came out 22 December.

At the end, as the song played out I thought, 'Oh fuck'. I knew that shit wasn't supposed to happen. Sam hadn't wanted it out. But he was dead and I guess the label figured, 'Why not?'

When we got back to LA, the first place I went was

Sam's house. It was only a couple of weeks since I met up with him in his pyjamas. Now the place was a madhouse. There were people everywhere. Sam's wife, Barbara, was totally shocked. I didn't know her well, but I wanted to talk to her, just to say something, anything. But everyone around her said she wasn't seeing anyone.

The day of Sam's funeral was sad. It was an early afternoon. The Rev Charles preached the service.

There were a lot of stars. Not Sammy Davis Jr, though. I wondered why Sammy didn't show. Ali was there. He was mad. He was waving his hands around and told anyone listening – and that was most – that he didn't like the way Sam was taken out. Or the punishment dished out to Franklin. If it had been Frank Sinatra, he said, the cops might have done something. He was saying the establishment didn't care about Sam living or dead.

If there was a person with a magical spirit, Sam was it.

Sam had charisma and a very special way to get into people's hearts through his songs and his music. But Sam wasn't just a singer, he was a leader, and he was getting ready to try to shake things up, to raise the consciousness of the world and stop prejudice. If he hadn't been cut down, he probably would have become a politician.

I cried throughout the whole service, but even with my eyes full of tears I could see Sam didn't look like himself. He looked like he'd had a real hard life. I guess it was the brutal way he died.

A lot of the musicians from Sam's band were in the same car with me. I was crying my eyes out, serious sobbing, until somebody said, 'Man, shut the fuck up.' Then the complaining started. 'I didn't get this' or 'I didn't that.' Another guy said, 'Sam promised me a gas station.' Even Cliff had a beef. It seemed like everyone thought they'd been stiffed.

That bothered me. I thought, 'Christ, is it going to be like this when I die?' I didn't want that. It didn't seem like real friends talking. Their mood also made it hit home that Sam was dead. It was like losing my mom and dad at the same time, that's how badly I was affected.

No 11 December gets past me. As the date approaches, it builds up. The nearer it gets, it starts to feel very dead inside me, like a funeral. Then it arrives. I'll watch the whole day go by and notice everything that happens.

Each time I get myself on my own, nobody around. I might go out to the beach, some place quiet like that where I don't hear no phones or nothing. Then I'll walk around and I'll think, 'Damn, I wonder what Sam would be doing right now.'

I might laugh at when he used to tell me to get myself a little martini so I would look grown up. Have a cigarette on the go. Or the first drink he got me started on, Jack Daniel's. 'Just sip it,' he instructed.

He had a huge influence on me. I knew it. I admired him. I know I wouldn't have gone through all the drugs and booze if he had been alive, because I promised him. I told him I would never run astray. And I would have stayed that way if he'd lived.

I was always afraid to sing Sam's songs. I ran away from

them. I always thought they talked about me. 'A Change Is Gonna Come' made me so humble. You know you can't be real cool on stage if you bat your eyes and tears come out. That's what happens if I think about Sam. So I thought, 'Let him sleep.' Then I asked myself, 'How can I stay away from someone who influenced me so much?' Staying away from him, his songs, that made me uncomfortable too.

After Sam died, Barbara had him put in a crypt. You needed a key to get in there. She gave me a key, and she had a key. She said, 'Let's buy our crypts now.'

'Now?'

She said, 'Bobby, you have to get ready for death'. Maybe, when I was ready. But then? I wasn't much into my twenties at that time.

However, Barbara went ahead and bought us each a place either side of Sam. We never got to use them ourselves.

CHAPTER 8

WOMAN'S GOTTA HAVE IT

A little after Sam's funeral, maybe a few days, I was at my apartment. JW Alexander swung by. He told me he knew how I felt about Sam, but the show had to go on. He said he'd spoken to RCA about making me a star, how I could write and sing. 'We got to keep this thing going,' he said. 'Just keep going to keep the doors open and selling records. That's what Sam would want us to do.'

Sam had wanted me to go back with my brothers, but his death spelled the end of The Valentinos.

Oh, man, I didn't know what to do. I wasn't thinking about any of it. Not launching a career, nothing. I told JW there was no way I could do that. 'I can't think about it, I can't believe Sam is dead,' I said. 'I can't think about nothing at the moment.'

Alex then cut to the chase. He said he had $65,000 of the record company's money in an account under his and Sam's names and he was willing to put that up to back me. He said, 'You could take the band and keep working.'

I skipped around to see Barbara as soon as he was out the house and laid the 65-grand story on her; what JW had said. She dismissed it out of hand. 'Well, I don't believe that,' she said. 'And number one you wouldn't know nothing about it.' She treated me as just a young kid – I guess I still was.

'That's nice of you to tell me,' she continued, 'but, number two, I know everything about my husband and you don't have to tell me.'

'All you have to do is check it out,' I suggested.

She thought about it. Kept thinking about it. And then she called the bank. The account was there. Because it was in Sam's name, they agreed to turn it over to her. After that, Barbara began to gain some sort of confidence in me. I was still the kid on the block, but I'd gained her respect.

I didn't hear what she said to JW about it. Or what JW had to say about that; he didn't say nothing to me, but I figured he must have been pissed. Just before Sam died, he had stumped up the cash to buy everybody in the band new instruments. Barbara had tried to find out who still owed on them. Recalling their reactions at the funeral, I advised her to forget it. 'Let the band have them,' I said. 'They earned them.' A gift from beyond the grave so to speak. So I became the middleman between her and Sam's old group. That got me closer to Barbara.

A few months after Sam's death, The Valentinos surfaced uncredited on the Checker Records recording 'I

Found A True Love'. Then we went to Chicago and Chess put out a couple of records, 'What About Me' and 'Sweeter Than The Day Before', in October 1966.

Friendly had already bailed out and then so did I. After that, The Valentinos didn't go anywhere because they didn't have enough energy. Harry was very laidback, but Curtis was even more so.

One of the things I missed most was going on stage with my brothers. I missed, more than anything, being able to sing with them. I didn't see it as a blessing then because we were just doing it, singing and playing. It was natural. I didn't know anything else. After working the business for a few long years, though, I realised there was nothing to compare with singing with those guys. You can make it alone, but the group is so different. It has got so much to give and one person can't give what all of you can give together.

I don't know what we would have done if we had stayed together, but it would have been great. All those minds working for songs and ideas. Egos play a big part whether you're brothers or not.

I'd heard Barbara was seeing someone else – it had probably been going on a while. Sam played around behind Barbara's back a bit; more like a lot. Sometimes he said, 'I'm gonna get a divorce.' Sometimes he might have said that around people that maybe he shouldn't have said it around and it probably got back to Barbara.

I went up to the house. There was a guy there, name of

Al. A bartender. Al was standing in the middle of the kitchen, Barbara in the doorway. After Sam died, I don't think Barbara had too many friends. She was feuding, always had a feud simmering on the side with the Cooke family. Now she was by herself, she had a lot of money and I figured she was wide open to be taken. Al could have been there to play Barbara. Either way, I thought he was no good for her.

What bothered me more than Barbara playing around with a guy was that Al was wearing Sam's ring. His watch, too, and Sam's robe. The man was barely cold and Al had his stuff.

Al was a big guy, six-two easy, and around 250 pounds. Just huge, muscular, not an ounce of fat. He made about two of me. But this ring thing pissed me off. I told him to leave – and leave Sam's stuff on the side.

We stared at each other. I may have only been 20, but already in my mind I wanted to be in the position where Al was at. Al didn't look happy. He glanced over at Barbara and she said, 'You heard what the man said. You'd better go.'

Al slipped off Sam's stuff and left.

Barbara seemed amused. 'You just run off my boyfriend.'

I played it cool. 'He had no place here,' I told her.

'Well, you got to take his place now.' She said it just like that.

I didn't know what she meant at first. It seemed pretty fast. I told her she could call me at my Inglewood pad any time.

Not two days later, she was on the phone. Told me there were some songs on Sam's tape machine that he'd been working on, but she didn't know how to work it. 'Would you come out here? See what's on the tape and tell me what you think about it.' She added, 'There might be something you could use.'

I thought nothing else about it. OK, I thought one thing. I was always a little scared going up there to the house – at night – after Sam passed away because I believed in ghosts. I knew Sam well, but much as I loved the man I would have been freaked out if I'd seen a vision of him standing in the living room.

So I promised Barbara I'd get up there the next day, during the day. Barbara was having none of that. She wanted me up there around eight. She told me she had some other people coming over. Turned out it was Rene Hall, the arranger who had worked on 'A Change Is Gonna Come'. When I arrived, Rene was already there with his wife, Sugar. Sugar and Barbara were real tight.

We put away a few cocktails and a little something to eat. The evening was up and running. It felt comfortable that someone else was at the house. Rene rapped about music, and the girls were chatting about stuff. After a while, I kept seeing Barbara giving Sugar these looks. Just sly little glances. Sure enough, Sugar suddenly announces she and Rene were a little tired. They were off. I went to go with them, but Barbara reminded me about the tape recorder.

This machine was in a little office, off the side of the house. We went out and I could see it was easy to work. Just on and off. Nothing to it. I was bent down, adjusting the tapes, trying to make out like it wasn't so simple a child could have operated it. I could feel Barbara standing close behind me, so close I could feel her body.

The rest happened like *The Graduate*. All those years I never got no pussy, but now here was Barbara Cooke – Sam's wife – blowing hot in my ear. I was scared shitless. My hands were shaking, fiddling with the tape.

'What's the matter? You scared of me?' she asked.

'Oh no, Miss Cooke.' I was always polite. 'I ain't afraid of you.'

'Yeah? Well, I like a man to look at me while he talks.'

I kept fiddling with those tapes and buttons. The next thing I know, she's gone. I had a breather from the tape machine. But she was back within a beat, this time dressed in a heart-stopping red robe. It went all the way down to her ankles, but wasn't exactly tied tight.

Something started to happen. Maybe if I'd been a little more experienced I could have controlled what followed, but I didn't. I had no control. Then, I told myself it felt right – it was supposed to happen.

We kissed. We went into the house. I don't know what happened to those songs. At that moment, I couldn't care less. I was going to step into Sam's shoes. I felt that I was taking care of Sam, too. I wouldn't let Barbara down. No player was going to fuck her over. I'd look after her, the house, the kids. That was a big promise.

We slid into the living room; we're on the couch, on the table, on the floor. And she asked, 'Why don't we go in the bedroom?'

'Do we have to go in there, Miss Cooke?' Still called her Miss, used to it.

She told me off again. 'Call me Barbara, Bobby.'

'OK, Barbara.'

'Let's go into the bedroom.'

'OK.' I tried to sound like I was cool, but my heart was right up there in my throat.

After our first night together, Barbara said, 'I want you to come back every day.'

I saw that a lot of stuff Sam left was sent to his brothers. But I kept an old briefcase of his and Sam's binoculars, which he used when he went to the races. They were brand new, but he'd scraped his name on the rim – Sam Cooke. Still got them.

I also kept hold of his make-up kit. Sam had always been complaining about the raggedy dressing rooms so he had this case made up with everything in it. He also had a pair of golf shoes lying around. Barbara told me he'd tried a couple of rounds, found it too slow and left the shoes at the back of the closet. I had no use for the golf shoes.

Barbara also let me try out some of Sam's clothes for size. We were about the same build, him and me. They fitted. I didn't own a suit, and now I had dozens. Dozens of Sam's suits. I always admired the way he dressed.

Things started to go fast. Barbara's plan: she was going to help with my career. I was going to help her.

101

'It don't look right now you coming up here all the time because people are going to be talking,' she said.

I said, 'They already talking.'

She said, 'Why don't you marry me?'

'I don't think I'm old enough.'

Barbara was around 30, 31. Ten years older. I was shocked, the way she asked me. She said, 'Well, you ain't got nothing else to do, you got no job, you ain't working. There ain't nobody booking you anywhere.'

I thought about it.

'Why don't you marry me and make it legal? And then people won't think we are just sleeping together.'

'OK, I'll marry you, Miss Cooke.'

'If you call me Miss Cooke one more time... my name is Barbara.'

'OK, OK, Barbara, let's get married.'

I packed up what little I had and moved up to the house on Ames Street.

We went downtown the next week, down to the LA courthouse. All the press was there, photographers, TV cameras, lights, the whole ball of wax. It was jam-packed, it was chaos. Like a major event. There were a lot of dumb things said. Stuff like: 'He could be almost her son' or 'Did you already go with her?' Barbara said nothing and she told me to say nothing.

My oldest brother Friendly Jr came along to give us support. Barbara's sister, Emma, came along too.

We were ready to go. But *I* wasn't. I wasn't yet 21. Had a week to go. Oh, man, I was totally embarrassed.

The press didn't want to wait around – or come back a second time. They told me to call Cleveland and get my parents' permission. I said I wasn't going to do that. Barbara said, 'Call your parents.' I was my own man; I didn't need my parents' consent. Wasn't sure they'd give it neither. I knew my father wouldn't agree. I told them all it wasn't going to happen that day. We got back in the car, waited a week – 'til my birthday – and then went back. I was just 21 years and one day old when I got married the first time.   It was two or three months after Sam's funeral. That's when the problems started.

Barbara had a crazy five-year plan. She said, 'If you promise to give me five years, I will give you a lifetime. You know, whatever you need to do, I just need you to walk with me here.' She needed that support. 'I need you to walk with me through this estate; you seem to know a lot of these people and you can read them and tell me who I should talk to and who I can trust. I trust you, Bob. You're not out to get anything.'

That was true. However, I had been planning to be with her forever, not five years, but she was telling me just five years, that's all she needed. 'I wouldn't put you through it no more than that.' She said that right from the beginning because she thought that I was going to leave, like it was too good to be true.

Then we started getting the hate mail. We were getting all kinds of dirty stuff through the post; someone even sent a box with a doll in it. Like a baby in a coffin.

Barbara had a baby by Sam called Vincent. He tragically drowned in the pool at the front of the house about a year before Sam's death. He was only a toddler when he died.

Sam and Barbara argued about having a fence put around the pool at the front of the house. Sam was against it, said it would ruin the landscape. He argued that in addition to Barbara there were two maids around to watch over and look after the kids. Apparently, it wasn't enough. Vincent, who was around two, went through the doggie door, got in the side of the pool and drowned.

I guess the doll was supposed to represent that. It was sick and nasty. It seemed no one liked the fact that I had married Sam Cooke's widow. And I mean *no one*. Not my folks, not my family, not my friends. Man, it was lonely. It started getting like a lot of pressure too.

Nancy Wilson, a good friend of ours, invited us to one of her gigs. She told the audience there were some friends in the house, breathed into the mic, 'Say hello to Barbara Cooke...' And the audience went, 'Ooo!' and applauded. ...and her man, Bobby Womack.' And the audience booed.

Many times we would go to events and – after seeing all the filthy looks and catching some vicious verbal spite – I would get out and go sit in the limo until it was all over. I got tired of dealing with all the negative attitudes, but I didn't want to run away from it.

Sam's family had a real problem with me marrying Barbara. It was no secret, Sam's brother Charlie told me. He told me he thought I was trying to fuck over Sam. He called me. 'Man, anybody else could have married Sam's wife, but you. Sam loved you, man. If you ever come to Chicago...' The threat was left hanging but I knew it was meant.

Now, Charlie wasn't a pussy. He was the kind of cat who would die for Sam. I saw him take a knife off a guy, who tried to stab Sam. This kid, a stagehand, had a flick knife and was always talking about cutting Sam. There were always fuck-ups around so I didn't take much notice. One night, Sam tried to bring some people backstage and the guy wouldn't let them pass. Sam told him to get the fuck out of the way and he pulled his knife. Charlie jumped right in there, took a stabbing, but knocked the guy out. The next time I saw Charlie, he was in hospital with tubes sticking out of him.

I figured if Charlie was going to do something I wanted to go and get it done, get it over with. I thought, 'Whatever they got to do, let them get it out of their system.'

Barbara and I flew to Chicago. We checked into the Roberts Motel and I called Sam's brother. I told him, 'I'm here. We're in 2112.'

He said, 'OK, I'm on my way, brother.' And hung up.

In the motel room, Barbara busied herself loading bullets into a pistol. Now Barbara had a mean streak in her, she would react. She thought I was crazy walking into their territory, but I knew I had to get it over with. I didn't want to be worrying about what could happen some time down the line. If Charlie made his move now, the chances were he wouldn't fuck with me again.

Once the gun was loaded, Barbara stashed it under a pillow and went into the bathroom to put on her robe. I took the ammo out and put the gun back. I didn't want to be creating the trouble. What would it look like if she shot Charlie? They would say Bobby Womack went to Chicago to kill Sam's brother. I may as well have committed suicide if that had happened.

I was scared waiting. I could hear the second hand on my watch tick down the minutes. I could hear Barbara in the bathroom humming to herself and making herself beautiful. I felt cold. Then there was a knock at the door. That chilled me some more.

Charlie showed with his two brothers, David and LC. I opened the door. No one smiled, but Charlie said, 'Oh, man, you showed up. You got a whole lot of nerve, haven't you? You little fucker.'

I said, 'Yeah, I'm here.' I went to shake his hand, and Charlie punched me.

He beat me so bad – so fucking bad – my whole head was swelled up like a melon. My teeth came through my lip. He beat me unconscious, then he hit me conscious again. He broke my jaw, the whole bit.

I lay on the motel carpet and looked up at him. I could see him hitting me: after a while, I didn't feel a thing.

I didn't try and fight back. I figured he was mad and I wasn't. But Barbara came out of that bathroom screaming. She thought they were going to kill me. She made a grab for the gun under the pillow and pulled the trigger. It just clicked and Barbara couldn't understand why. 'I'll be goddamned. This stupid motherfucker.' She looked down at me, bloody on the floor. 'You took the bullets out the gun?'

I knew she'd use the gun so I saved Charlie's life by unloading it. Charlie knocked her down too.

There was a guy in the room next door. He banged on the wall, then he called the cops. Charlie went to run out but the door was still half-open and he ran right into it and bust his head open.

When the cops saw the state of me, they said Charlie would do time. I didn't want that. I thought if it was my brother I might have done the same thing. I was willing to take my beating like a man and get on with it. They put Charlie in jail and told me to press charges. I went down to the station house and told them to let him out. He was sitting down there looking at me so hard. I said, 'Let him out. I don't want him locked up.' Then I walked away.

Two strange things happened after that. A few years later, I played Chicago. Charlie showed up to the gig with David and LC. Charlie didn't want any bother this time around. He said, 'We just came to give you moral support.'

A long time after that beating, maybe 20 years later, I was in a barber's shop. I heard this guy whisper to the barber, 'That's Bobby Womack.' The paranoia that I had felt after Sam's death flooded right back. Then the guy asked if I remembered him from Chicago. He was the guy in the motel room, banging on the wall, the guy who called the police on Charlie.

Barbara was trying to sort out Sam's affairs and the estate. She was headstrong, but she didn't know too much about the business side, like publishing, and I tried to tell her how it worked. One thing I advised her was not to sell the publishing, Sam's publishing. It would be a steady earner, and a big one. But some things she just wouldn't listen to me on. It was: 'Look, I'm running the show now. I just wanted to ask your opinion.'

She was making big decisions, but not always making them with a cool, clear head. JW lost interest in Sam's label SAR, so in 1965 Barbara dissolved the company. It got worse when she found out that Sam owed a whole bunch of taxes.

Barbara used to get up every morning, six o'clock on the nose, fix a coffee with a little brandy in it. She also used to put $50 in my jewellery case, every day, just so I had some spends, a little cash in my pocket. It was easier than doling it out over breakfast. I felt terrible, but I had no money because no one was hiring me for gigs – my name was still mud after the wedding – and I hadn't started writing that many songs by then. I told Barbara I'd pay her back. I had no idea how.

To add to all the other shit I got after marrying Barbara, the army called up. I'd just got married, and now with the Vietnam War raging, Uncle Sam came calling.

There was no history of our family being in the army. Not my father, his brothers or my brothers. I was reluctant to break that duck; I didn't want anything to do with Vietnam. I thought I'd gone through enough shit just to end up in a lousy war trying to dodge a bullet.

The army wanted me to take a medical. I made some

plans to ensure that didn't go so well. I ate a bar of soap. Some guy had told me the trick was not to eat for a couple of days and then munch on soap. It ran my blood pressure sky high.

I went down to the army induction and was sick as a dog, throwing up all over the floor. My blood pressure was so high one of the docs couldn't understand why I wasn't dead.

When they gave me a drink of water, I started coughing up bubbles from all the soap in my stomach. That got their attention. They knew I was shirking and I spent the day down there doing all their exercises as they checked me out. I passed. One of the sergeants said, 'Look at this guy, you really are a cheapskate that you should pull this stunt.'

I said, 'I don't want to hurt nobody. I can't do it.'

This cut no ice. 'Oh, yeah? Well, you're going, Womack.'

Told them I was a Muslim, name of Bobby X. That didn't matter to them none. They knew I was bullshitting anyway; I had no ties to the Muslim brothers. The army sent me home and told me to be ready to leave for boot camp in a week.

I told Barbara what the country had planned for me – fighting out in the jungle. She hadn't planned this when we got hitched. 'What are we going to do?' she asked.

I wasn't finished yet. I had another idea: the next day I went and bought a dress. Didn't stop at the dress neither – that was a little polka-dot number – I got the whole outfit down with black stockings, high heels, a nice wig

109

and a big hat with a little veil. When I slapped on the lipstick and a bit of mascara, I looked pretty hot.

When I went back to the recruitment centre to show off my new look, they thought I had the wrong department.

'No, I'm Bobby Womack.'

The attitude was: 'Why do you think you want to go to war, ma'am? Or is it sir?'

Flashing my false eyelashes at the sergeant, I said, 'I just want to be there to help the soldiers.' I gave a cute corporal a wink and a flirty toss of my golden mane.

I was trying to hit on every guy in there. Told them I wanted to go through the part where everyone strips off for a full medical examination, but they weren't buying this nut job either. 'Mr Womack, it won't work, you were just down here the other day and then you was a Muslim,' said the recruiting officer. 'Womack, we are about sick of you. Take that shit off, go back home and come back here dressed like a man. You are going in the army.'

'I got a career going,' I protested. 'I just had a record, man, I just got married. I can't go.'

Oh, man, I was going crazy then. All my best moves had fallen flat.

Next thing I knew, I had another doc examining my feet. He asked me, 'How can you stand on those feet?'

I wasn't listening.

'Your feet are flat, they look like pancakes; you'll never make it through basic training,' he told me.

Flat feet. I laid it on thick, told him I couldn't run and could barely walk.

His next words were music to my ears: 'Go home, son, you won't be any use to us.'

I would have run out of there, but I still had that dress on and I couldn't even walk too good in heels. When I made it home, I told Barbara I wished I'd known I had flat feet. After using the other scams, the army now had it on record that I was a soap-eating, sexually ambivalent Muslim.

After that little experience, the army must have figured they'd seen enough Womacks. They never called up any of us brothers. Turned us all down.

The only one in our family to join was cousin Henry, who helped get us to California when Sam called. He got married before he left so he would have something to come home to. He couldn't face Vietnam straight. He told me some guys were getting ganja, heroin, all kinds of shit. He figured he would be OK with drinking, but when he came out he was a drunk. Had to be drunk all the time and wore his army gear all the while.

Henry said he'd never seen so many dead people. He'd stood next to a brother talking, looked away and the next thing there was nothing there but a leg. Man, you don't forget something like that. And, when he came back, his wife had left him for another man.

Sam's death – the way he had died – scared me bad, but Barbara and I had only been married for a short while when I found myself at a motel with a girl. It was the same situation that Sam was in and I could feel him looking down on me. He would have said, 'Don't be stupid, Bobby.'

I was nervous when I took that chick into the room. I was so worried I would be recognised, so scared I couldn't think properly. Then I didn't want to take my pants off, or my shoes or my socks. Practically fully dressed. I didn't want to be caught out like Sam. I made sure I could run out of there in a hurry. Not be left in just my shorts.

And all the while a voice in my head told me, 'Oh, that was just how it was for Sam. Go ahead, it won't be like that.' At the same time, I also thought, 'Man, what are you doing here? I don't need to do this. It's not like I'm going to die if I don't do it.' These two conflicting voices and I just wanted to scream, 'Leave me the fuck alone. My dick is hard and I want to fuck.'

All that messed with my mind. We started making out and then another voice came in, asked me where my keys were at.

I told the girl, 'Hold up, baby, hold up, hold on now.'

I started to feel for my keys in my pants, real slow. I hoped they were there. They weren't. I panicked.

She asked what was up, then told me not to worry. 'We'll just do it and then let's go,' she said.

Didn't work with me. 'Nah, I've got to get my keys now.'

We never got around to fucking. I searched around a bit and then went out to the car. I was so paranoid that someone might recognise me I locked the keys in the car. They were swinging from the ignition.

Barbara had another set, but I couldn't call her because she would have asked what the hell I was doing in a motel. Then I thought about being exposed in the press:

112

SINGER WOMACK PLAYS AWAY.

I took a brick and busted the car window out, grabbed my keys. Then I called Barbara. I told her someone had tried to break into my car – thought that was pretty clever. She asked me where I was. I said I was on the way home, they knocked the window out but then saw me coming and ran off. Barbara said, 'Hurry home.'

On the half-hour drive, I looked at that story and thought, 'That fucking around, it just ain't worth it.'

So for a while, a long time, I didn't play around. Just didn't fuck around at all. My dick went on vacation. The way I saw it, if something took my mind away so bad that my dick wouldn't get hard then it wasn't worth it.

CHAPTER 9

CRYING TIME

Right in the middle of all the hassle after I married Barbara, I got a call. Somebody told me Ray Charles was putting a whole new band together. He wanted me to audition. Ray had been cleaning up, trying to kick heroin and he didn't want any musicians around him who were still using. This was late 1965.

I don't know if Ray knew about the pressure I was under. It hadn't let up. Nobody would give me a break. I recorded my own tracks and I would take them to radio stations. 'This is a hit record, Bobby,' they promised and then they threw the record right in the garbage can. The jocks would break the record right in front of me and toss it in the garbage. Just because I had married Sam Cooke's wife. It was a boycott.

I was untouchable, but Ray probably figured he could use that. At 21, he knew I didn't have any kind of habit that he could feed off. So I liked that; Ray Charles offered me a way out. I'd never met the man and he gave me a gig.

Ray auditioned a lot of guitar players. I didn't want to go through all that, but I didn't have many – or *any* – choices right then. He didn't know if I could play his music. I knew I could.

I sat at the audition with my guitar and a book of music in front of me. The book was about an inch thick. I didn't open the book. Ray walked in. He shouted out a bunch of numbers, like 48, 92, 31, 15. Then he said, 'These are the songs we're going to play on these page numbers, just so you know the way the songs are going to come.'

I still didn't open the book, just looked ahead – waiting. Someone must have pointed that out. Ray said, 'You know, young man, you ought to open up your book.'

I said, 'I don't read music, Mr Charles, I play by ear.'

He laughed. Then spat out 31.

The other musicians found the right page in their music books and started up on song 31. I left the book unopened, but joined in. I was going along, playing the music. Suddenly Ray stopped the band. 'Second trumpet player. You are flat, tune up.' The guy tuned up.

Ray kept switching songs, going from one number to another, trying to lose me, I'm sure. I kept up. I was in there playing. He stopped the band. 'OK,' he said to me, 'just you and me play.' Then to the band, 'See what kind of ears this guy really got.'

Ray launched into one of the songs in the book and off we went. Now he could hear me playing without the rest of the musicians and still couldn't believe it. 'You haven't played these songs so how do you know where the chord is coming?'

'I have to know because I don't read.'

He didn't know how I did it, but he was impressed. For the first time since I played with Sam, I got a gig, although Ray had a warning. 'My music is way more complicated than Sam Cooke's stuff.'

To play in the Ray Charles band, all the new guys had to get themselves kitted out in the house style. Man, that was the opposite of slick.

To save money, the suits were handed down. Every musician who left Ray's band or retired passed their suit on to the new guy, so these outfits were well past retirement age. They were high water pants, but high water hadn't been in fashion that century. Also, the last guy who wore my jacket must have weighed 300 pounds. It was like making a suit for George Foreman and then cutting it down to my size. It was a whacky mess; the coat was supposed to be beige, but had faded yellow, there were patches in the ass. There were nametags in it going back to the stone age.

I never wanted to walk out on stage because I was real skinny and the pants would be up to my armpits and the jacket hanging way off my ass. I'd go out front and whisper, 'Mr Charles, Mr Charles. Can I just sit?'

'No, stand, young man. Go out there, they like you.'

But when I got to the microphone with this clown suit people would laugh. Ain't that a bitch they were looking at my pants. Behind me the band would be laughing, too, because any breeze out on that stage would blow my pants out, making it look like I was jigging.

Blind man Ray, he didn't understand why everyone was laughing. I told him again, 'It's the suit, man. It's the fucking suit.'

His reply was always the same: 'Don't rassle with it. If you rassle with it you gonna get tired and, if you get tired, you get frustrated, and if you frustrated you can't play, and you can play. So wear that suit. Think of all the great musicians who have filled it and you are filling in for now.'

'Yeah, but I'm the motherfucker had the suit belonging to a guy with the clap.'

Oh, man, it would itch. I'd play the guitar scratching.

Ray was a womaniser too. He'd chase women harder than anybody, always hitting on the backing singers. One day I heard he had a girlfriend coming to see him. He told me how beautiful she was, gorgeous figure, long legs. She showed up and, man, she was plug ugly.

Sometimes I couldn't figure Ray. He was blind and obviously couldn't tell if an ugly broad told him she was hot, but he would and could play chess. That impressed me. All the band would try and beat him, but he'd kill everybody at the game. I couldn't work out how he knew where the chess pieces were. I'd lived and worked with the Blind Boys, so I knew a lot of moves blind people had, but I never figured how Ray could do that.

A blind man playing chess was one thing, but flying a plane – now that was different.

The first time it happened it tripped me out. I got

aboard the rig we were flying on. It seated about 40, and all the band was there. It was Ray's own plane. And I saw him up front in the cockpit clicking all kinds of switches and flipping buttons. I guessed the pilot let him do that as a favour and then took over.

I didn't say anything 'cos no one else did. I thought, 'They'll tell him to come back and take his seat soon.' And, sure enough, Ray ambled back, buckled up and the plane began to taxi down the runway.

However, as soon as we hit air, the buckle was off and Ray raced up the aisle towards the cockpit. I said, 'Where's he going? He never runs like that when he's going on stage to play the piano.'

The pilot handed the controls to Ray. One of the band filled me in: 'Ray always takes over the controls.'

That freaked me out. 'Oh, Jesus me. Dear Lord,' I prayed. 'There's a blind man flying the plane. This is nonsense.'

'You don't need eyes to fly a plane,' the trumpet player told me.

'You don't need eyes? So why are there windows in the cabin?' I looked out at the clouds and then screwed my eyes shut tight and prayed some more.

Man, I couldn't sleep for thinking about our flights between gigs. I thought if I told someone they would think I was crazy. A blind man was flying the plane. I had attacks about that. And it was regular; a couple of times I thought about tipping off the airport authorities. Tell them, 'Man, Ray Charles is driving the plane.' See what

119

kind of reaction I got from that. They'd probably put me in a mental hospital.

I told Barbara I didn't want to play a gig. She said I didn't have to play, we had enough money. That wasn't the reason, I told her. The reason was Ray was planning to fly the plane to the gig and we were all expected to be on board. I was a nervous wreck worrying about it. Barbara told me to have another drink. Or maybe I had had enough. I said, 'I ain't lying. He will fly the goddamn plane.'

I'd heard that Ray had tried to drive this old Caddy one day. Just decided he fancied driving it home so he ordered his driver into the passenger seat, got behind the wheel and set off. He hit some dustbins, two or three cars, but luckily no people, before the cops stopped them. Ray swapped seats with the driver and he took the rap. So I asked Ray once why he thought he could fly a plane. You know what he said? 'Because it's mine.' Later, I heard it split in half before take-off. Ray Charles was going down the runway in Miami and the plane cracked like a walnut.

The flying was one reason I quit Ray's band. There was another reason, though, and that was Curtis Aimey. I had to room with old Curtis and he was always having seizures.

After my first experience of Ray flying, I was just glad to get to the hotel. But we had to double. I drew Curtis. Someone in the band pulled me aside and told me to keep a spoon handy.

'A spoon? What do I need a spoon for?'

'You need it for Curtis,' he said and then he hipped me

about the fits and that a spoon would stop Curtis swallowing his tongue. I just got off a plane with a blind pilot, then they told me Curtis had seizures. And I knew we had to fly again the next day.

Naturally, somewhere down the line Curtis had a seizure. He was a big old guy so I was scared half to death when I tried to get that spoon under the roof of his mouth so he couldn't bite his tongue off. I tried to wrestle with him and he almost chewed my fingers off.

Curtis would always want the motel window wide open, even in winter. He'd push it open, snow would fly in the hotel room and I'd close it. He'd push it open again – it could be blowing a blizzard – and I would close it again. He said he couldn't breathe. I said I couldn't sleep, not with no gale blowing through the room.

We'd fight over that. Terrible rows. One time we took the fight on the plane with us. I threatened him, 'Next time I tell you to close that window, close it or else.'

'I want it open,' whined Curtis.

'You push it open again, I'll push you out of it.'

Ray had taken a break from flying to beat one of the band at chess. But he listened to this bitching session. And Curtis wouldn't drop it. 'You push me out the window, you going with me.'

'You can carry that damned spoon yourself. My hand is swollen,' I raged. 'I didn't come here to be no nursemaid; I came to play my guitar.'

Eventually, Ray cut in, told us to shut it. He didn't want to hear no more about it. Naturally, he did. From me.

'Young man,' Ray said, 'I don't want to have to tell you again.'

'Hey,' I said, 'everybody wants to be my daddy ever since I been on the road. When I was in Sam's band, they all tried to be my daddy. I couldn't get no pussy; I couldn't drink. Now I'm in another motherfucking band and it's the same shit. Ray Charles is my daddy. But no one is telling me what to do. I got to put a spoon in his mouth, I'm freezing to death most nights and I got a blind man flying the plane.'

Ray said, 'Now I'm going to slap you if you say one more word. You will get the worst whupping of your life.'

'Well, if you slap me they are going to say it was terrible how that young boy whooped that blind man. He didn't see the punches coming.'

Ray didn't like that.

I said, 'If you slap me, you won't be able to slap nobody else.'

He was silent for a moment. I could just hear the roar of the engines. Then, he said, 'You're fired.'

I said, 'Man, I ain't fired. No, sir, I quit.'

I got off the plane, went home and didn't speak to him for a week. But, thinking about the money, I called him to apologise. 'I was mad at the time, the way I acted on the plane,' I said. 'But I'm a professional and I'm still on top of my game. I'm willing to play with you, Ray, as long as you want me to play with you.'

He said, 'Bobby, I respect you for that.'

I never saw or heard from Ray Charles again.

CHAPTER 10
FLY ME TO THE MOON

I was canned by Ray in 1967. Jobless and potless again. Fuck. I was going nowhere as a solo artist.

I went to Minit/Liberty Records. They asked if I had any songs. I told them I'd got a whole bag full of them. Hang on to them, get yourself in a studio and record a few, the record guys said. I told them I wanted a guarantee. The record company said, you bring us back a hit album, sell some records, we'll give you all the guarantees you want.

I went down to Memphis. Wilson Pickett had hipped me to the place. 'Bobby,' he said, 'there are some white boys down there; if you closed your eyes, you could not tell they weren't black. Those fuckers can play.'

Those fuckers were playing at a place called American Sound.

Now Memphis was hot. There was Stax, and across the street American Sound, which was coming strong. Stax was too locked up for me, but American, run by a guy called Chips Moman, had everyone cutting there. It was just a funky old hole in the wall in a real bad section of town, at the corner of Thomas and Chelsea. But it had a vibe; it all worked. I headed there.

After breaking from Stax in 1962, Moman had hit Nashville playing guitar on some country tunes before returning to Memphis to start American. He got himself a strong house band, with Bobby Emmons on keyboards, Tommy Cogbill on bass, Bobby Wood the piano player, drummer Gene Chrisman, and Mike Leech who also played bass and arranged strings.

Life was too easy for me staying in Sam's old place in Los Feliz. It was robbing me of all my ideas. I could pick up that $50 that Barbara left on the dresser every day and not go hungry.

'I need to feel hungry again,' I told my wife. 'I've nothing that I've worked for myself.' To get back to the ghetto was what I needed; get young, get hungry. And start producing again.

So I flew down to Memphis and found myself the cheapest fleapit in town. The Trumpet Motel, one rackety old room, one bed, single and well used with a tiny kitchenette. Junior Walker, BB King, they all stayed there and there were no distractions. Just the music.

So I asked if I could sit in on the sessions at American. 'I'm good,' I told Chips.

'That's great 'cos we got Aretha coming through and then Wilson Pickett the following week.'

I dug that no one bothered me there. No one asked me

about Sam Cooke or nothing. It was just musicians hanging, playing the best they could and showing each other their tricks. They just knew me as Bobby Womack, guitar player.

I figured I could really get my schooling from American. It felt right. It was the place to be, I loved the atmosphere and there was a little soul-food place around the corner. Perfect. We cut every day Monday through Saturday, Sundays we were off, but even then we'd be in the studios shooting pool.

I was especially good at the intros. That's what made Moman and the others notice me. And I started making good money. They called me cold blooded the way I would slip a guitar break in to make a track sing. Give a crafty hook to the intro, something people don't forget.

I played on everything. I mean every-fucking-thing that came into town. Aretha Franklin, Jackie Wilson, Joe Tex, Joe Simon, King Curtis and Dusty Springfield when she was recording *Dusty In Memphis*.

We didn't work like studio musicians. We really got into the artists that Chips brought in, especially if they were songwriters. We would try to play for them, to become their band. We would also try to produce, so it was like you had five or six producers helping the act.

Every time we went into that studio, we thought we could produce a No 1. And we did. Something like over 100 Top 10 hits in just five years with that same rhythm section. I was always worried that the band members would quit right when we were cooking on a track. They'd go for a coffee break and I thought they'd be calling it a day.

They said, 'Man, why you keep looking like that?

'I think you're going to quit and we're hot right now.'

Chips told me to cool it. 'Man,' he said, 'they ain't going to quit.'

Elvis Presley must have heard about us, or at least his people had. He called around to cut sides for *From Elvis In Memphis*. We weren't that impressed. Yeah, man, Elvis is coming, so what? The guy had had his day, so we thought. It was like, no big deal. But then he showed up. The back door opened and in walked Elvis and we all backed up a step. He looked great.

He had some kind of charisma that was pretty powerful. And then he had his posse, always matchin' him. Lightin' his cigarettes, there'd be seven or eight guys flicking out their lighters, click, click, click. Checking Mr Elvis had enough to drink or eat. See Mr Elvis wasn't too tired. Well, they got kicked out of there by Chips pretty early on and we could get down to some business.

We'd hang out with Elvis, chat about school, Memphis, anything. Just a bunch of guys shooting the breeze, talkin' shit. Someone would name a song and we'd play it. Elvis wasn't the kind of guy to do another take. He had gotten away from the thing of staying up all night in a studio, and by then was used to having everything programmed.

It was like he was on stage all the time, he had all his outfits on. The big collars, all the fancy shit. He dressed up

126

all the time. He told me he had to dress that style to be Elvis. That's what people expected of him, to be on, to be Elvis. I thought, 'Shit, I bet he doesn't dress like that at home. I bet he's in his shorts watching the TV.'

Elvis was good in the studio. There was always a little bullshit behind everything, we had a laugh. He also bought everything, all the beer, all the food. He even brought in a bunch of songs, but it was all pretty bad. Stuff that sounded like show tunes. They played a demo and Elvis asked what I thought.

'Man, that's bad,' I told him. And it was.

Then Moman pitched 'Suspicious Minds' and 'In The Ghetto' to Elvis and he loved them. So that's what we did.

I worked on Aretha Franklin's session for the album *Lady Soul*. I was playing guitar with a cigarette in my mouth. Cool. It was 1967. The track 'Good To Me As I Am To You' turned out to be one of my most embarrassing moments. When it came down to the blues, I was never a blues player, but I was doing my best.

The producer, Jerry Wexler, said he was looking for something else. He asked if I had heard of The Yardbirds. I said no. He said, if it was OK by me, they'd like to get this guy. Get him to play the blues parts. So I said fine, no big deal. But I was thinking to myself, 'Fucking white guy going to come in and play the blues and tell me, Bobby Womack. I'm supposed to be the man.'

Eric Clapton was very polite. He had his little guitar and asked if he could use my amp. I told him he was doing the gig, he could have my guitar if he wanted. He didn't. He started to play. There was nothing I could say. I was looking at him. That motherfucker could play guitar. He could *really* play. It reached my heart, so I knew it.

A lot of us blacks have a hard on about white men not having the blues, but Clapton played so hard and I was staring at him and people were looking at me. I'm sure they thought, 'What do you think now, Womack?' I stared so hard at Clapton watching him play tears welled up in my eyes. I didn't want to bat my eyes because I knew the next minute I would be crying.

I went to the bathroom, washed my face and came out. I told Clapton it was a pleasure meeting him. He said, 'I'm only trying to do what I can do.'

And I said, 'You sure did.' He knew how to play the blues and I could never bend the notes like that.

My father used to say, 'They [white folk] don't have to be around us and we don't have to be around them.' I was already totally confused about everything I had been taught when I went to Memphis because all those guys in the studio were white. When we ate, they asked for black eye peas, cornbread, buttermilk on top of the cornbread. I said, 'You like this kind of food?'

They didn't know what I meant, that I thought they were eating black man's food. But after seeing Clapton I started thinking, 'What made a guy play like that?' He must have earned it.

All of my albums were basically white guys playing on it. I never wanted to tell anybody because I wanted to keep that quiet. This was soul music and people said white people can't do soul. I got more education playing on those sessions in Memphis and at Muscle Shoals, Alabama. I wanted to say to those white guys, 'How did you learn to play black music?'

My own record for Minit was going slow. I'd got myself down to nearby Muscle Shoals in Alabama when Wilson Pickett rolled into town from New York. I hadn't seen Pickett since I'd been out on the road with him.

Whatever Pickett said, he stuck by it. No matter. He was tough, but also a lovable guy, a sweetheart, would do anything for you. He didn't trust a lot of people, however, and – mostly – I don't think he trusted himself.

I wrote a string of hits with him; Pickett ended up recording 17 of my tunes, including 'I'm A Midnight Mover', 'She's So Good To Me' and 'I'm Sorry About That'. So I got to thank him for something.

He called me Womack Stack. I forget why.

Pickett came out of Prattville, Alabama, born a few years before me on 18 March 1941, a Piscean too. I remember him from the gospel-harmony group, the Violinaires, then he joined the Falcons in 1959 and came up with the song 'I Found Love' a couple of years later. That was a big, big record. He left them and went on his own. Jerry Wexler took Pickett to Memphis where he cut 'In the Midnight Hour', which hit in 1965.

Pickett was more comfortable on stage than anywhere else, apart from maybe fishing. He loved to fish, go out on his boat and get away from everything. He was also the kind of guy who liked to hunt; you could tell he was a country boy, no question. He sang, played guitar a little bit, too, and he blew a mean harmonica. He could really blow. He had a unique sound and kept a big band; sometimes carried around 15 musicians, five horns, keyboards, couple of guitarists. I followed after – went on the road with him for a few years.

I knew I was a hell of a musician. I had a rep as the number-one guitar player, and I liked it the way Pickett had it, the way he sounded. I wanted what he had; I wanted it to sound just like that on my records.

One of the prettiest songs I ever made was 'I'm In Love'. Pickett kept telling me to record, but following Sam's death and me and Barbara hooking up I was still taking flak from everyone in the business, including radio stations. I told Pickett, 'Hey, man, they see my name on a record and they throw it in the garbage; they don't want to play my records.' All the jocks were Sam's old friends and they thought I had betrayed him.

Wilson was very talented. Came from a real religious family, all gospel. Once I got to know him, he was a nice guy, but moody. Very, very moody. He wasn't a man that you could mess with. You could joke with him about something one minute and in the next he'd be on you and trying to kill you.

That's why they called him Wicked Pickett. Everybody called him Wicked because Pickett wasn't the kind of guy who thought about what he did. Self-destructive. He kept a lot of stuff secret. If he got mad, he got mad and was always running somebody out of his house.

He had a thing against the system, like a lot of black artists, but most of us didn't express it as much or make such big waves. If you were finding success, you thought, 'Shit, I'm getting along, so fuck it.'

But Pickett, he didn't hold back on nothing. He had a fight with anyone who was part of the machine, anyone, any time. I mean *anyone*, even me. I could always tell when he was getting ready for his thing and I should get the hell out the way.

This was typical: he looked at me real hard – maybe he was a little drunk – and said, 'You like my old lady?'

'I think she's nice,' I replied. I didn't know what else to say. But she was nice, a beautiful woman.

He said, 'I know she's nice, *do you like her*?'

'Well, you know I...'

Once he'd got me to admit I liked his wife, he kept on at it. 'What does "like" mean, Bobby?'

'Like means...'

'You like looking at her?'

'I jus' like her as a person...'

'What kind of person do you want her to be to you?' Then he'd start in: 'You motherfucking, dirty bastard, you trying to fuck my old lady?'

I know he loved me but, if someone, maybe the press, gave me a little bit of attention, he would snatch it away. So he might have said something like, 'You want to do an interview with Mr Womack?'

'Yep.'

'You want to do an interview with him? He works for me.'

He also said things like, 'I don't want you talking to those people, Womack. People come to my dressing room, don't talk to them, don't talk to them about nothing.'

I'd tell him, 'They wanted to know about the album.'

He wasn't impressed, just wanted to make a scene. 'I don't care,' he would say and turn away.

There was always something like that and he could embarrass me something bad. Fortunately, we never had any physical bust-up because I would walk away or talk my way out of it. I knew someone would get hurt.

So there was always an undercurrent of tension and violence around Pickett. I used to wake on the wrong side of the bed, just wake up evil and mad at everybody. An hour later, everything was normal and cool. I don't know what that was, but I tried to work on it and work it out.

Pickett didn't. He was different; he was a violent man. I know he came up really hard, but I never dug into his life that deep to find the reasons that made him vicious. Why he always wanted to fight, always thought someone was trying to steal from him or someone was trying to talk behind his back.

I've seen him jump on people, somebody in his band, hit them across the head with a guitar because they missed a note. I know he beat one of his musicians once.

132

Later, when he was sitting around someplace, the guy he had attacked got his revenge; he picked a poker up out of the fire and ran straight at old Pickett. Someone shouted a warning, Pickett turned his head and the poker went into his eye. I couldn't believe it. Afterwards, Pickett had real problems seeing much out of that eye.

There was racial tension when black musicians toured in the sixties, especially in the south. The rednecks didn't like us going into their white areas; sometimes those guys thought musicians would be poaching their women. So that was always an explosive mix – Pickett's temper versus the racist white boys. The first time I joined Pickett's band he asked me, 'Bobby, have you got a gun?' Oh, man.

Pickett always carried one. Inevitably, we were heading for trouble. He told me that, said trouble's around the corner in some town out on that long road. 'Last time we came through we kicked a little ass,' he told me. 'None of the boys got hurt.' And then, 'Everyone has got to have a gun. Ain't gonna take no gamble because if we have to come out fighting we come out fighting.'

I listened to all this and thought, 'Are we gonna play a concert or we going to get killed?'

Some other time and some other place, a club owner offered Pickett a couple of thou just to walk through his place after the band had played the set. $2000. Play the theatre and then walk through. Easy for most folks, not Pickett.

He got me and the rest of his group around him and laid it out to us. 'Now, we're going to walk through this

133

club,' he explained. 'I'm going to be at the front walking real fast. If any of you motherfuckers stops, something bad will happen to you. Just keep walking; I don't care what nobody says.'

And he came through that door into the club, walking so fast you'd think he was in a race. Walked straight through, out the back door – he was gone in a flash – and got into his car. He asked the club owner, 'You got that $2000 for me?'

The guy had thought he'd stop and sign a few autographs, press some flesh, ask the punters, 'Hey, how you all doing?' He said, 'Mr Pickett, I asked you to walk through my club, not run through. Nobody saw you.'

When Pickett was in a good mood, I'd try and explain that he'd go a lot further if he didn't act like that, treating everyone mean. He'd nod. 'You're right, Womack,' he'd concede. 'But I'll tell you something, man, if you're fucking with me.' And, of course, it never made much difference to how he acted.

One thing he did take advice on was setting up a publishing outfit. I got sent a royalty cheque and Pickett got sight of it. He wanted to know how I got more money than him. 'Hey, I'm singing the song,' he said. 'You're getting more money than me.'

I told him it was publishing. 'Man, that's what pays the writer,' I said. I was the writer. 'It's important.'

Pickett had some kind of deal where he had been paid something like ten grand a year not to have a publishing company. I don't know how that worked, but he was adamant he wanted to get one going. He got me to go into Atlantic Records to meet with the boss Ahmet Ertegun.

I was there to help him negotiate. He looked like he was going to walk through the door. That's the way he walked all the time, real hard. The label was very uptight that I was trying to school Pickett about that, but the publishing company got formed. They said, 'Fine, Pickett, we have no problem with that.'

He said, 'It's going to be different from now on, anything coming in and my publishing is going to be all over it.'

They knew you don't mess with the Wicked.

Yeah, Pickett, he always wanted me to be right there with him. He trusted me. There was a reason for that: sometimes he had to.

He always avoided interviews, had some kind of problem with them. Like me, he'd quit school early and always had a paranoia that the journalist would try and humiliate him, worse if it was on TV, so he avoided doing interviews. He couldn't always escape, though, and just before one he told me he had difficulties reading and writing. That was devastating to me. I said, 'I understand perfectly now, you're a king when you're up on that stage and you remember these lyrics. But to be pushed into another world because of what you do, man, it's hard.'

It was the same mentality with banks. Didn't trust them. None of us did. I was probably in my mid-twenties before I had my own bank account. I used to keep my money in my shoe.

The way I figured it, if it's my money I keep it. I paid cash for cars. I didn't want to fork out for anything that I had to pay on the stump because I figured my dream would disappear one day. If I paid cash for shit, it would always be mine.

Managers, advisers, whoever, they would advise me to lease a car. Told me I could get some tax back. I said, 'Lease, does that mean they still own it?' I always paid cash so no one could touch what I got.

Pickett went a similar way; actually, he went Pickett's way. When it came to someone looking after his business, he would always get someone that he could totally dominate. He thought it was better to have them scared, knowing how much they knew. 'Don't you ever think of putting your hand in the kitty.'

I asked him one time what bank he dealt with. He told me the bank door. I didn't know what he meant until he opened up a closet in his house. Instead of clothes, it was stacked full of money – all the way up to the very top.

'Goddamn, this is crazy. Do you know what you could be making on the interest?' I said.

Pickett knew. 'I made this. I picked cotton and shit like that and I ain't never going back. I keep my money right in there. Man, I ain't putting nothing in the bank. You know what that is? That's the white man figuring a way to steal back what he gave me. You put it in the bank, they move it.' Then, when he saw my eyes bulging at the stack of notes, he told me, 'You had better lose interest in what you seen in that closet or I'll kick your motherfucking ass.'

136

Eventually, I had to leave Pickett's band. All the fighting, the violence, it started to bother me. I was brought up the tough way, but Pickett was a little harder. And it bothered me seeing him hurt himself or if someone beat up on him. Things were happening all the time like that.

I think what scared me the most was when we were driving with a real pretty girl one night. He had picked her up from a gig, and she said she wanted to hang out. So we did, him driving around all these dark country roads in the middle of nowhere.

It suddenly turned ugly. Pickett stopped the car and told the girl to get out the car; he put that girl out on the highway. He said, 'Well, you hang out here on the country road now. You think you can hang in all this darkness?'

Man, it was dark, cold and lonely there. Pitch black, middle of nowhere. She would have had to walk ten miles to the nearest town – if she knew where that was. I said to Pickett, 'Hey, baby, don't do this, man.' He didn't want to know. He said, 'This bitch is getting out here.'

Probably the last straw, the incident that made me think I would be better without Pickett's company, was when he left his band to drive all the way from Baltimore to New York – with no brakes.

There was about a score of them, in a truck, not a bus, more like a furniture van. And it had no brakes. The musicians told him, 'Mr Pickett, we don't think we will be able to make it.' It was a long way. He said, 'Oh, you'll make it all right. Get home the best way, you can use the emergency brake, that's what it's there for – an emergency.'

It was snowing and they couldn't slow down or stop safely. I was up front, riding in a car with Pickett. He'd told me to ride with him. 'I want you to be out here with me. I want you with me because you're talented, you got more talent than those motherfuckers; you don't deserve that, Bobby.' The band, cramped into that truck, followed our car and I could see them through the rear view – I could hardly bear to watch – slip sliding all over that highway.

To see those guys all crunched in that truck was painful. It was a death trap. I asked him why we didn't get two or three at least to come and ride up in the car with us, but he thought that was a crazy idea. I thought, 'Oh, man, you're going to get those guys killed.' But I couldn't do anything about it and Pickett waved his hand and said, 'Bobby, this is my shit.'

I thought then I'd rather know Pickett from a distance than be up close around him. A little while after the business with the truck, we were sitting together drinking a beer. He would always give me encouragement. Told me something along the lines of: 'Man, when you played that song last night, when you hit me with the licks on the guitar, man, that's what made me sing. I'll never find nobody like that...'

I knew I had to tell him I was leaving, and I started crying. 'Pickett, I know you cut my songs and everything, but I can't sit here and laugh like I'm happy. I'm not happy.'

I told him I had to go. I wasn't brought up his way, he was hard. He had a heart, but it had been fucked with so much. Pickett was cut up about me leaving, but it was the only way I was going to survive.

No doubt Pickett helped me. I'll always have a deep love for him because he stuck by me when I was trying to get going and because he recorded my songs, gave me a break, and everybody needs a break.

After that, Pickett would change his telephone number real regular. No one could reach him. I would call around, end up going to people who owed Pickett. 'This is Bob, I need to get Pickett's number.'

I would put a call into him. He said, 'Who's this?'

'Bobby.'

'Bobby Womack? How'd you get my number, man? How'd you get it. Tell me how you got it.'

'Pickett, I called...'

'You know you can always have it. You know I love you, man.'

Then he'd call the people that gave me his number and cuss them out.

That happened so often that to the day he died I didn't know how to reach him.

At Muscle Shoals, Pickett got into the studio and never got out. I waited. And waited. I wanted to get in there and record my material.

Then I made a big mistake. The reason Pickett was slow was he had no songs. I started showing him mine, all of them. Man, I had a few and Pickett had none. 'So why don't you just let me sing all them songs you got?'

'OK,' I told him. 'But I'm keeping the publishing.'

He said, 'Fine, I just need some hits.' This was 1968.

He'd take one, play it, nod and ask, 'Got any more, Bobby?' There was probably half a dozen in total. He asked, 'You sure you don't want to record this for yourself?'

'Man, I got plenty of them.'

But I ran out. I just sat there every day watching them record. He was cutting all of my stuff. He recorded his album *The Midnight Mover*, and left town. Left me with no songs and I still had my solo album to do. I also had my record label on my case. They would ask when I was going to start my sessions.

I always told them the same thing. Tomorrow. Then tomorrow would become the next day, then the next would roll around and I was still dry. Not one fucking song. We'd be sitting around throwing up ideas and, man, I was trying to think of something. Anything to pop out. It was like looking in the well after a dry summer. Nothing, and I was cursing Pickett. Why did he have to come into town?

Liberty turned up the pressure, kept checking on progress – or lack of it. Somebody told them I was looking pretty burned out and that I'd just given Pickett some great stuff. They didn't know that 'great stuff' was the songs I'd promised them. I told them, 'I just gave Pickett a few ideas.'

One night we were sitting around the studio and I still

had no songs. But for some reason, I started to play 'Fly Me To The Moon'. It just came to me. Everyone was asleep, but I kept playing this song.

The other musicians gradually woke up and got on the tune. They asked me what it was. It was like a joke to me, but they didn't know it wasn't my tune. They didn't recognise it. I took a Tony Bennett song and put a beat on it. I thought, 'How could you sing fly me to the moon so slowly?' Flllllyyyyyyyyy-meeeeeeee-tooooo-the-moooooooon. You'd never make it there that slow. So I picked the song up a bit, gave it an up-tempo beat. To get to the moon I thought you needed a bit of speed. So I gave the song that 'fly de duh, me de duh, to duh, moon, de da duh'. That sounded more like it. At that speed, they might actually make it.

Then I came up with 'California Dreamin''. The whole album was just about covers. I thought, 'Man, Liberty are going to be pissed.' And they were. The record company fell through the floor when they heard what I had cut. They asked about all the new material I'd said I had.

'I gave the songs to Pickett.'

They were unimpressed. 'And you give us this shit? This is a Tony Bennett song.'

A few years later, I was coming out of a movie theatre just as Tony Bennett was going in. In the foyer he said, 'I liked what you did to that song.'

'Yeah? You serious?

'Yeah, it was tasty you didn't mess it up,' he told me. 'You did a great job.' He thought it was very hip.

141

They put out 'Fly Me To The Moon' – my version – and it was huge.

CHAPTER 11

MORE THAN I CAN STAND

Barbara was a very witty, sharp woman. She could, and did, take a lot. She could endure. But the thing I realised — something I thought she already knew — was that she and Sam were a pair. They lived each other, they really did.

So she used to cry a lot of nights. She had these very bad headaches and used to bang her head against the wall. I asked her how long she had been doing that. She said a long time. 'Bobby, it's like a train running through my head.'

She said she'd seen Vincent in the pool in a dream and I felt so bad for her crying about her dead son. She was close to cracking up. Always thinking about Vincent. I said, 'I could get you pregnant again.'

'No, my tubes are tied, I lost babies. I can't do it no more,' was her response.

What made things worse was she was always talking about how my dick never seemed to go down. And she was right. I'd just be about to go on stage – 'Ladies and gentleman, all the way from Cleveland, Mr Bobby Womack...' – and my dick would be up. I'd have a swim and come to get out of the pool and, oh, no, there it was. Hard again. I thought, 'Damn, what is wrong with me?' My dick always seemed to be ready for action and I had to think about ice cream, anything, until it went down.

It got so bad Barbara said it wasn't normal and took me to see a doctor. She said, 'Listen, Doc, can you give him shots to take his nature away?'

He was having none of it. He took me aside and counselled me not ever to let anyone give me shots. He warned. 'It [not getting it up] is going to come soon enough.'

So, thankfully, I didn't get those shots and I kept on at Barbara that I could give her another boy and soon enough she was pregnant. It was the one thing I could give her. It was a boy. We called him Vincent too, after the son she had and lost with Sam. Barbara spoiled him rotten.

Nothing seemed to change the ill will people felt about me, though. Everyone still saw me as the guy that moved in on Sam's widow. It got so I was always nervous, shell-shocked. I needed something to inure me to all that bullshit. I just didn't know what. Until I was introduced to coke. OK, I'd never done drugs. So why not start? I had fear and I was told coke was comforting. It was, and I needed that. When I took coke, I didn't care what people said about me. I walked up to them and smiled. 'How you doin', sir, have yourself a good evening.'

Coke was my escape, and to up the protection I started wearing dark glasses. I wanted to be able to see out, but didn't want anyone looking in. If they did, they would have seen a boy half-scared to death.

I took coke with me everywhere I went and I stayed fucked up. I chopped out fat lines like there was no tomorrow. It didn't matter then what people did or said to me. I went to Chicago to perform and after every song the audience wouldn't applaud. They would just sit there. The DJ on the bill asked them to give it up for Womack. Nope, they wouldn't. Fuck it. I got my cocaine to give me a lift.

I turned Pickett on to it, too. I don't know why I did that. He saw me once and said, 'Bobby, why you putting that powder up your nose, man?' I told him it was how I coped. I said, with cocaine, 'I can write, I don't fear no man, I don't fear nothing, I don't even feel nothing.' Pickett laughed at that. Told me I was weird. A weird motherfucker.

We tried it together. This might have been in Memphis when we were up writing some of those songs. We were up for three days straight and Pickett turned to me and said, 'Bobby, I ain't going to sleep, I ain't tired, I ain't hungry. And all we are doing is writing hits. Let's go and get a whole bunch more of this shit.'

I really believed I was giving him something good because it was something that worked for me, but then I heard about him getting busted for coke possession in the early 1990s and then I didn't feel so good.

So I did blow for 20 years of my life. Two decades of

snow. People would tell me I would be better off without it. What the fuck did they know? They weren't living on the end of all that hate.

To add to the paranoia – and this brought me all the way down – my brothers were reluctant to be around. They knew the threats were out there against me. They didn't know what to do, but without them I was totally alone, all by myself, and, because my father and mother had been against the marriage, there was no family in my corner. My mother had said, 'I don't think you should marry that woman, you don't know nothing about that woman. That's Mrs Cooke, that's Sam's wife.'

I said I was getting married anyway. I had thought I wanted to be a man – this made it so I would have to become one fast.

This guy Gene was my dealer. He was laying coke on me every day. I was spending $700 a week with Gene on coke. Barbara took care of the bill. He would bring it up to the house. I would tell Gene I didn't want it no more. He said, 'Nah, man. Here take it.' Then I'd pour it out on to the glass coffee table in the lounge, chop out half a dozen killer lines on that smoked-glass top and snort most of it before he was at the bottom of the drive.

Barbara was always pushing me to record Gene. I told her the guy couldn't sing. He had no voice, not that I'd heard anyway. She was adamant. All his life he'd been a dope dealer, but he'd got close to some entertainers, and now he thought he was one.

I took Gene to some of my shows. I even wrote a song.

My first group was the Womack Brothers. From left to right, my brothers Cecil,
y, Friendly Jr and me. Curtis is at the back

m: My father, Friendly.

Top left: This was Friendly's first group, The Voices of Love. My father is front left.

Top right: Uncle Wes and Betty Jo inspired me to write 'It's All Over Now'.

Bottom: My brother Harry, aged 10, a girl named Shirley Parker and me, 11 years old. This was taken in July 1955.

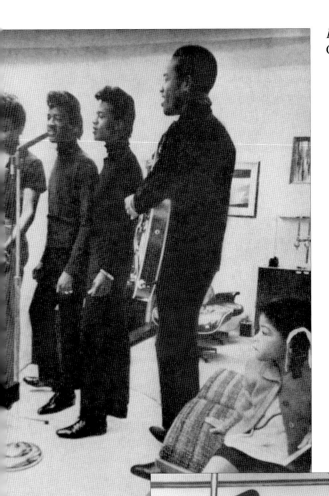

Left: The Valentinos in Sam Cooke's home studio.

Right: With Sam Cooke in [s]tudio in 1961. From [t]o right it's Cliff White, [ ] Gardner on drums, [ ]n guitar and Clarence [ ]ey, with Sam in [c]entre.

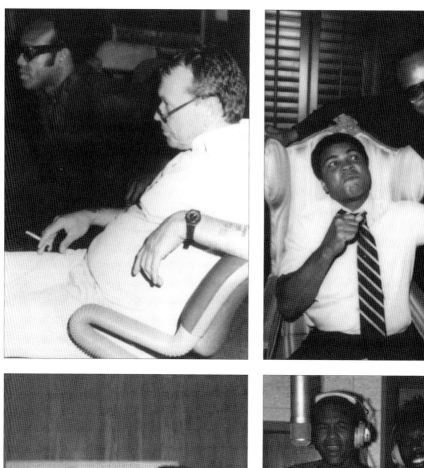

Top left: Chips Moman was the record producer from American Studios. He'd worked with Elvis Presley and Wilson Pickett.

Top right: Clowning with Muhammad Ali.

Bottom left: Me with Ray Charles…

Bottom right: … and with Wilson Pickett.

Top: A 1970 family shot. From left to right, Vincent (the son I had with Barbara), Linda and Tracey (Sam's daughters) and Barbara, Sam Cooke's widow and by then my wife.

Middle: The house Sam Cooke bought on Ames Street in Los Feliz. I moved into there with Barbara. The pool at the front is where Sam's son drowned.

Left: Mick Jagger, Ronnie Wood and me.

Top: Me, Mary Wells –
she was the singer who
was a real hit on
Motown when she was
young – my brother
Cecil, who married
Mary, and another one
of my brothers, Harry.

Middle: With John
Lennon and friends.

Right: My son Vincent
and me with Marvin
Gaye.

eft: Clive Davis was the head of Arista Records.

ight: Patti LaBelle, who played on *The Poet II*.

m: In the studio with Jody Laba, the mother of my sons Cory and Jordan.

This was me with Sly Stone shortly after he'd got out of jail one time.

Jesus, that was a fucking low. Called it 'You Got My Nose Wide Open'. I must have looked like the biggest joke in the world. I tried to sell the guy as a singer to a couple of record labels, but they weren't buying.

'Bobby, this kid has nothing,' was the drift. 'He may as well be throwing up.' Finally, they found out what the catch was with me and Gene. Gene supplied the tonic.

I was using the coke and drinking to hide behind what was really happening in my life, but somehow I was still writing songs. Some good, some not so good, but Barbara did me one favour. I had come up with one tune called something like 'Oh How I Miss My Baby'. I don't know what got me on to writing that, but Barbara saw it and asked straight, 'Are you unhappy here?'

'I'm not unhappy.'

'Then why would you be singing about "Oh How I Miss You"? Who do you miss, Bob?'

I didn't know. Maybe I had Ernestine in mind, but I think I was just trying something out. Trying out some emotions, ones that I hadn't yet experienced. So I didn't know how to answer Barbara.

Barbara told me that if I really saw myself as a writer I had to be true. I shouldn't make up stuff about missing someone if I wasn't missing someone. Write about love if you're in love and hate if you hate. 'Be true to your art, don't make it up,' she said.

'There are a lot of people who miss their baby and I am just trying to let them know that I understand how they feel.' But I knew it would sound fake.

147

'You can't let them know you understand how they feel unless you've been there. Have you been there, Bob?'

From that time on, I made a commitment to myself that I would only write about what I had experienced. I gave Barbara credit for that. 'Write about what it is and what you seen,' she said. And I did.

We made a good couple like that. The age gap sometimes got in the way because she had been around, was much more worldly, and she was always aggravated by what she saw as my boyish ways. I wouldn't ever make a scene, always had a quiet 'Excuse me?' when Barbara would use 'Hey, you!'

She thought I was naive, and if somebody did something to put one over on me I would generally put up with it. Back then, anyway. Barbara wouldn't. She would shout the house down until she had everyone doing it her way.

Also, Sam cast a long shadow. His presence hung over that marriage. No matter how we looked at it, we had got married right after Sam's death and because of Sam's death. While he was alive, we'd barely exchanged two words. The marriage and everything else only came up after Sam's death. That only added fuel to any fiery arguments. And we had a few.

'Why are you here?' she'd shout.

'Because of Sam.'

'Sam? Hey, I want a man to love me, not my husband.'

'I never loved you, I loved Sam. I only married you so I could protect you and these kids. I loved Sam.'

Barbara couldn't believe it, but I told her, 'Don't play dumb on me. I never loved you like that. I loved everything that was part of Sam and you guys were. I just felt sorry for you.'

That brought a deathly silence. And then she exploded: 'What did you say?'

The way I looked at it, it seemed like we never loved each other. Barbara just said, 'Let's get married,' and we did. I had nothing else to do, I had no job. I had nothing going. I tried to explain it to her. I said, 'I didn't do this to hurt Sam, I did it because I thought Sam would appreciate me standing in the way of anything that could go wrong with the family. It's like taking up a fight for your brother.'

That made her angry; that I was there for Sam, not her.

One night we were with a couple, Jim and his girl, Pinky. We were hanging at their place, having a drink. Suddenly, Barbara turned and asked if I was hip.

It was totally out of the blue, but I figured I was so I told her, 'Yeah, I'm hip, babe.'

She asked again, 'No, really, are you hip?'

'Sure, baby. I'm hip.' I wondered where this was going. 'I hope so, sport.'

Then she laid it out for me. She wanted to go with this guy Jim. She said, 'I want you to switch and be with his girlfriend.'

I'm surprised. Was I that hip? She thought I was scared. I told her I wasn't. Disappointed, though. 'Oh, baby,' I thought, 'we were going to be husband and wife, not part

149

of a swinging party.' What I said was, 'I just done nothing like that.'

'Well, let's just try it one time.'

So I lay there with this girl Pinky and we're trying to get it on, working some moves, but I couldn't get nothing going. The more she worked on me the more my dick stayed hidden. It had disappeared. It just wasn't happening and across the room I could see this guy on my wife and I couldn't handle it.

Pinky didn't help matters when she announced to the party, 'I think Bobby is too square. His joint, it don't matter what I'm doing to him, it ain't there any more.'

I told them I couldn't do it; I couldn't handle it, I guess, and upped and walked. I headed straight for home, but I wasn't in the place two minutes when Barbara came flying in behind me.

'I love you,' she said. 'I was just fucking that guy.'

What was I supposed to think? That was all right then?

Barbara was still slipping me that $50 a week — she was taking care of me all right. I was totally under the thumb; she had me on a lead, like a dog. Her idea was to build a club where I could sing every week, like my own private venue and gig, but I told her I gotta make it on my own.

Then a cheque popped through the post, about $30,000. It was my first piece of money from royalties and all the other shit I had been doing. I finally got some money of my own and I wanted Barbara to have it, show that I could provide for her and her daughters, Linda and

Tracey, to contribute and put something back. I wanted to be the man of the house.

Before I could bank the cheque, Barbara went to Chicago. While she was away another letter dropped on the doormat, but this wasn't royalties. This one was addressed to my wife. It was a bluff envelope, kind of legal looking. I opened it. Wished I hadn't. I saw from the paperwork it was related to an apartment in LA and some furnishings for it. The person the apartment had been set up for was the dealer, Gene. A cosy fuck pad.

My eyes fired red. I was furious. More than furious, I was hurt. I'd been made a fool of. Fucking Gene. Got me fucked up and then made a play for my wife. I broke down crying. Then I called Gene and told him not to come back up there with any dope or I'd jump on him.

So the thing boiled down. I sat there. I was totally fucking angry. Then I got Barbara on the horn. I told her straight, 'You hurt me for the last time, baby. I'm leaving.' We rowed on the phone. We rowed about the girl she got me with, Pinky. We rowed about the drugs I was on. We rowed 'cos I didn't know where I was going with my music, where that was at. I was all screwed up.

She said, 'I love you, I was just fucking him.'

I'd heard that before. I thought, 'You should be fucking me. That's the best part.' What I said was, 'Hey, I am really through with you.' It ended when I slammed the phone down on her.

But hanging up had only ended that argument. I had

151

my marriage to screw up. Barbara had already done her part, what came next was my side of the deal.

Linda, Barbara's kid, had heard the row, probably seen the whole damn thing unravelling over the years. I sat there with the phone on my lap and she offered me some sympathy. Then she reminded me that it was her and me that was always supposed to be together: she had a point there.

From the moment I was under Sam's wing, Barbara had said me and Linda would make a fine couple. She would tell Sam, 'Save Bobby for Linda.' But Barbara didn't think it would fall like it did. I've blanked out most of what happened that night. After the row with Barbara, I told Linda not to worry about it and went to bed. I lay there thinking about that apartment that Barbara had rented Gene. How many other guys had she been with? What had she been doing while I was down in Memphis?

While I thought about that, the bedroom door opened. It was Linda. She slipped under the covers and got right up next to me. Linda was just a teenager. I swear I told her to go, but I didn't say it loud enough. Linda had my attention. What I recall is Linda's speech. It went like this: 'I thought Mom was saving you for me, but she took you and look what she made out of you. You're doing drugs and you drink.'

We could relate, we were young – even though I was married, I was still only in my early twenties. And the age gap between me and Linda was less than the one with Barbara. Both of us kids really.

'You don't even know what you are doing any more,' Linda added. 'You were always so young and innocent and look at you now, she's hurting you. She shouldn't do that.'

I told Linda that what we were doing was worse. She told me again that we were supposed to be together and that Barbara was too old for me.

'She doesn't want you. She's ruining you.'

At the same time as she told me this she gave me an erection.

I said we got to do this and forget it. Barbara will kill me. We made love. Maybe I got into it because I figured it would hurt Barbara – hit her back, with her daughter. Twenty minutes and it was over. So was my marriage, effectively. And when it was, Linda told me, she'd be there for me. 'You don't deserve this unhappiness.'

When Barbara got back from Chicago, things appeared normal on the surface. Nothing was mentioned, all brushed under the carpet, but things had changed. A lot. Linda started to treat her mom differently. Every time Barbara and I were together, Linda would walk in on us, interrupt us no matter was going on. It was like Linda was out to challenge her mom. Become her rival in love.

I continued to creep into Linda's room at night. I was supposed to be writing songs in the middle of the night, but really I was sleeping with my stepdaughter while her mother slept. It wasn't pretty. I was totally fucked up. I mean, everything was going wrong.

I got caught with my pants down, literally. That's when

Barbara put the gun on me. Had it right up against my temple and told me to get the fuck out of the house.

I was shaking, I couldn't put my pants on before I got shot – grazed. I hid in the garage and then ran on to the street in my shorts and flagged down the cops.

The cops took me back up to the house and took the gun off Barbara. She hadn't calmed down, but she didn't try to shoot anyone this time around. She told me flatly, 'I want you out this house.' She didn't get an argument.

I moved out. We divorced in 1970.

CHAPTER 12

FIRE AND RAIN

fter splitting with Ray Charles in 1968, I was on my own, fending for myself. I didn't have my brothers around me so I became a solo artist. I signed on at Minit Records. The first hit, 'What Is This', came along pretty quickly.

Then, after dumping all my best tunes on Pickett, I cut the covers 'Fly Me To The Moon', 'California Dreamin'' and 'I Left My Heart In San Francisco', the first two hitting big again in 1968. Then came the R&B hits 'It's Gonna Rain', 'How I Miss You Baby' and 'More Than I Can Stand' over the next couple of years.

Around this time, we had a little trouble out on the road, in Savannah, Georgia. I had put a band together and was constantly out touring, drumming up audiences to make those hits. We'd had a little problem with the equipment at one club – it wasn't there. There was some talk of cancelling, but a guy in the audience had other ideas. He had come into the club with a pistol and started shooting. Winged someone and they were lying in the aisle, bleeding. He then jammed a piece of metal in the door so no one could get out and started firing up into the ceiling, putting a couple of slugs in an old chandelier. Man, I was scared to death.

The crowd went quiet. You could have heard a pin drop. My guitarist ran off stage and locked himself in the john. I must have looked like a joke up there on stage – so I didn't stay. I ran right after my guitar player and knocked on that bathroom door, trying to get in, and waited for the law to arrive.

I liked to hang out, play some tunes. Musicians knew that and I'd get a call – see if I wanted to jam, rustle up some licks.

One day in 1970, I got a phone call. By the end of the same long day, the caller's life was ended, but the world had gained a beautiful song. Her name was Janis Joplin and the tune was 'Mercedes Benz'.

Janis called and told me she was recording her new album, *Pearl*. She had a request. 'Everybody tells me they have recorded at least one of your songs. I just want to say I've recorded one. Can you bring me a song?'

At first, I thought the phone call was a wind-up. I didn't know Janis, had never met her, and I wasn't heavily into her music. So I said, 'Janis Joplin, sure. And I'm John Kennedy.'

She had trouble convincing me after that. She got the album's producer, Paul Rothchild, to pick up the phone. Paul told me it really was Janis and she wanted a song from me. He made his pitch: 'She cannot do this album unless you give her a song.'

I was persuaded and I told them I'd be right down.

Janis was a prankster and when I rolled up she was sitting there with a straw hat and fiddling with a little bell. She shook her hand and it sounded. Ding, ding, ding. I wondered what that was for, but she was straight to business. 'Hey, Bobby. Have you got some songs for me?'

I had a whole bag full. One of them was a song called 'Trust Me'. She said, 'See this bell?' She rang it again. 'Play your songs, and every time I don't like something I will ring it.' OK, that was what the bell was for.

I started off with 'Trust Me'. I played it through, got to the hook and watched her hang. The bell stayed silent. When I got to the end, she was out of her chair. 'I love it, I love it, that's the song. Bobby, we got one.'

Man, I thought, it was going to be easy. I could clean up. 'Got any more?' she asked, but every other song I played after that the bell would come out and go ding, ding, ding. I must have sat playing for a couple of hours, going through nearly all my tunes, some by my brothers and a whole bunch that people had sent me to record. She would make me sing about half the verse of the next song and then she rang that bell like a town crier.

'Hey, don't you get it? I'm not going to cut any more of your songs. I only want to do one.'

'Fuck it,' I thought. 'She's getting ready to fuck with me.'

She asked if I wanted to stick around and play on the album. I didn't mind, I wasn't doing nothing else.

We showed 'Trust Me' to her outfit, The Full Tilt Boogie Band, cut it and wrapped it up.

All through the session, Janis was down. She was in tears some of the day and on the phone to her boyfriend. From what I heard, she wanted him to come out and see her, but he refused unless she wired him some money. I heard her scream into the phone, 'You always want money from me, that's all you want.'

I put my arms around her. Jimi Hendrix had only recently died and she was really in a fix about that. Crying and talking about death. I tried to console her, but she had hit the Southern Comfort heavily and the booze got in the way. People don't down that much just to drink. I didn't snort coke just to snort it. I wanted to snort the shit out of my life. It looked like Janis wanted to drown hers with booze. I'd only met her that day, but I could see the girl's life was in turmoil, a whole mess of trouble.

After the session Janis was pretty loaded, so she left her car, a Porsche with a bad paint job, parked at the recording studio. She asked me to give her a lift a few blocks up to her hotel on Franklin in Hollywood. I'd just got myself a brand-new Mercedes 600 so I was fine with that.

When I lived with Barbara, we would drive past the Mercedes showroom and I would point out the model. Barbara promised, 'I'll buy it for you.' But I wanted to buy that car for myself. Know that I'd earned it.

Barbara couldn't understand that I didn't want to be chauffeured around. I wanted to drive it myself and I just loved that car. When we split, I heard that Barbara drove past that same dealership and saw the car wasn't in the window. Out of curiosity, she stepped in to find out who had bought it. The guys in the showroom told her it was me. I had gone in one day with a briefcase full of cash and dumped it on top of the car. I drove that Merc right off the floor.

Like me, as soon as Janis saw that car she was knocked out.

She whistled. 'Jesus Christ, how did you get a fucking car like this? This is a fucking sharp ride.' We rode a couple of streets while she fixed a tune in her head and then started singing. A line just spilled out. 'Oh, Lord, won't you buy me a Mercedes Benz...'

Suddenly, she was inspired and the next line came tumbling, 'My friends all drive Porsches, I must make amends...' She was anxious to get right back in the studio again to lay the track down and ordered me to turn back. 'Let's go back, we're gonna cut this... "Worked hard all my lifetime, no help from my friends. So, Lord, won't you buy me a Mercedes Benz"...'

I reminded her the band had already split.

'Fuck it, turn the car around. Oh, Lord, this is great.'

She kept singing, making the song up as we drove around Hollywood, back to the studio. 'You play guitar right? Well, that's all we need. Me and you.'

We got back into the studio and Rothchild was about ready to leave. 'You forget something, Janis?' he asked.

She told him what was on her mind: 'We're gonna record.'

He told her to wait it out, until tomorrow. 'It'll keep; it's the Southern Comfort talking.'

But Janis was burning to get that song down. While Janis hummed the tune, Rothchild hooked up a couple of microphones. She was on an acoustic and I played my guitar, just the two of us; me trying to follow her. It was an easy song and when we got through she said, 'That's it.' And that was it – we split.

It was pretty late by the time we snuck out of that studio, around midnight. We headed back to where she was holed up again and I parked up in front of the hotel, a bundle of apartments set around an oasis of trees and plants and a pool.

Janis was in 105. Nothing too fancy, a bedroom with a couple of beds, closets, bathroom and a small kitchenette with wood cupboards and a table. We got comfortable. Sat up there, rapped about music, people we knew, the usual stuff. Just two rock'n'rollers checking each other out.

Janis had a little record machine in the corner of the room and persuaded me to get my album *Lookin' For A Love* from the car. She wanted to listen to it, but she thought it funny I carried my album around with me.

We cued up the first track and chatted some more. Janis had ideas about reaching out to black audiences and believed I was the guy who was going to help her do that. She said, 'I got a problem. Everybody thinks I'm trying to sing like Tina Turner. I don't want to be Tina Turner, I want to be Janis Joplin and I want to go out on the black side of town and be able to sing and show those people that I used to sing for drinks in New Orleans.'

I had a real problem crossing over, too. I figured the pop stations weren't playing my records – at least not enough. So her idea sounded sweet to me. A case of mutual back scratching. She pressed the point: 'You take me to the ghetto and I'll take you to the white side of town.'

I was in for that. 'Damn, that's great. Can I put it together?'

We figured we could set up a tour and do at least 15 cities.

Janis told me the kids at school called her ugly. She wasn't a looker, but I thought she was beautiful. It seemed like she couldn't accept that people would want her, unless it was for her fame and success.

She felt was that people saw her as a freak, but she was a free spirit. She was also a gentle person, very affectionate, and she just wanted to be loved. That drew me a lot closer to her. I understood how vulnerable she had become. It did cross my mind now we were back at the hotel that we might fuck. Ain't too many people got the chance to fuck Janis.

While I tried to put all that shit together, we got on to drugs. Talking about them. She was using heroin but wasn't holding. I had my cocaine. I had a little toot of blow and asked if she wanted some, but she said, 'Nah, I'm waiting on something else.' Then she asked, 'Why do you snort coke, Bobby?'

161

'Why do you do smack?'

She told me she became a user to bury all her thoughts and deaden her from the world. 'Because it lays me back, that shit speeds you up.'

My spin was: 'Both coke and H make you feel nothing, and if I'm feeling nothing I want to be up and not feeling rather than asleep.'

Then Janis got a call. She only spent a couple of minutes chatting and then put the phone down. She told me a guy was going to swing by right that minute. It was her connection, and he wanted me out. 'Hey, you got to go now.' I thought that she didn't want me to see him or at least see her take her fix. We kissed goodnight and she said, 'See you.' Just like that.

'OK, I love you.' We hugged.

And I left. I didn't see the guy calling with the smack. I wasn't paying any attention, just playing the day over in my mind.

I wasn't in my bed more than a few hours when someone called up to tell me Janis was dead, that she had OD'd. Man, I was shocked. I broke down and cried. I was the last person to see her alive, or last but one. Her dealer saw her last.

The police asked me for a description of anyone I saw in the hotel that night, but the only thing I could tell them was that I heard some footsteps.

A few years later, I was sat in my living room watching TV and a car commercial came on for Mercedes Benz with Janis's song. I turned to my girlfriend and told her,

'That's Janis Joplin. She did that song in my car. In my Mercedes car.'

I met John Lennon, but not under the best circumstances. Dr John was doing something down the Troubadour Club on Santa Monica. He called me up, told me to get my ass down there as there'd be a few stars I'd know; some of Fleetwood Mac were there and Lennon. So we were all hanging and jamming.

Then they started calling everyone up on stage. I got up there and made a grab for the guitar before everybody else 'cos that was the instrument I could play.

Lennon said, 'Hey, give me the fucking guitar, you cunt.'

I said, 'Fuck you, man.'

I got the drop on him and got the guitar. Lennon got on piano.

We were probably playing something like 'Johnny B Goode'. The piano was out of tune and he wasn't playing like he wanted to. He turned around to me and said again, 'Give me the guitar.'

I said, 'What? I'm playing the guitar.'

Lennon went crazy. I told him again, 'Fuck you.'

He gave it me back, 'Fuck you.' Then he got up off the piano to snatch the guitar off me, but before he did that he started to laugh. Said I couldn't even play it, I'd got the thing upside down.

Someone put him wise to who I was. Told him I was Bobby Womack.

I told him I couldn't play piano. I thought, 'Shit, I got to uphold my thing. I can't just give the guy the guitar just because he is John Lennon.'

Afterwards, Lennon came up and apologised. He claimed he hadn't known who I was and said, 'I'm John. Let's meet on better terms.'

I told him it was cool and we shook hands.

I never met him again.

Marvin Gaye was a genius, but he wanted to die like a hobo. Don't know why, I guess it was his genius, or madness. And he did have his freaky side. He told me once about driving down Sunset Boulevard making love to a hooker in the back of the car while his wife was at the wheel.

One time we were hanging at a studio on Sunset and he told me, 'When I go out I want to go like I came. With nothing.'

He did. When his time came, he was bankrupt, and owed the IRS some, and had been divorced from his wife, Anna.

A few weeks before he died in 1984, we had an album planned. His son, Marvin Gaye III, was putting it together. We talked about it and I turned up to the studio to record. Marvin's son was embarrassed. He told me, 'Marvin ain't going to make it tonight.'

Then Marvin called. He said, 'Bobby, how you feelin'?'

I said, 'I'm feeling good.'

'Yeah, can we book for another night?'

I said, 'OK.'

'I just got a little thing on here; there is too much going on at this time in my life. They won't let me be.'

I said, 'OK, what about Thursday night?'

'That sounds like a winner.'

Thursday night came and it was the same story. We got on the phone again and he said, 'I know you are going to chew me up'

'I ain't going to chew you up,' I told him, 'we're cool.'

That night he wanted to talk, to talk about life. His life. Marvin liked to open up a bit of a philosophical debate.

He said, 'Bobby, what's your father's name?'

I told him.

He said, 'Friendly? That means he is friendly, but what if your father's name was Gaye and your father was gay?' Their family name had originally been Gay.

I said, 'Oh, man.'

He and his old man had had a tempestuous relationship. Always arguing. The old man beat up on Marvin when he was a kid. Marvin told me his old man, Marvin Sr, used to tell him he wanted satin sheets, like women loved. He asked his son if he thought that made him gay.

We got into it some more that night on the phone. He wanted to tell me his problems. Some of those problems were with Motown and founder Berry Gordy. Marvin had married Berry's sister Anna, who was much older than him. He also figured that, when they had a fight, his wife would go straight to her brother and rag on Marvin.

I'd wanted to join Motown. When we were The Valentinos in Cleveland, we would have walked to the HQ in Detroit. At Mary Wells's funeral, Berry was sitting behind. I asked him, 'How come you didn't sign The Valentinos?'

He said our sound was too different – too gospel – from Motown. He couldn't embrace that. 'Man, some people you can't control and you didn't sound like Motown, you had a distinctive sound. You could tell a Motown act, I figured Sam would allow you to be yourselves and I couldn't make you be something else.'

I took that as a compliment.

Marvin told me about how he fought to get Berry Gordy to release 'What's Going On'. Berry thought the song was too political. The way Marvin told it, Berry said to him, 'You don't have to sing no shit like that. I mean, what's going on? Hey, if you know, keep it to yourself.' Marvin fought hard to put that record out.

He'd had a spell living out in Belgium in the early 80s, but he was at the end of his rope when he did 'Sexual Healing' in '83. He told me he had begged not to come back to the States to do a tour. He thought he would never make it back because he was too weak. I heard that towards the end he was walking around unshaven, in his pyjamas with an overcoat on top. And this went on for weeks.

He was shot in his mother's house. Marvin Sr shot him. They'd had another fight and Marvin went upstairs to see his mom. The old man followed up there with a gun.

Walked right in there and killed his son as he sat talking with his mother.

When he died, I knew he'd had his problems with taxes so I found out where his second wife, Janis, lived. She was much younger than Marvin; they'd got together in 1971. I didn't know her personally, but I had a few dollars and called her up, told her what Marvin meant to me, went out to the beach where she lived and slipped her a couple of thousand bucks. I knew everything that Marvin had left undone would be on her.

The last time I heard from him he asked what a nigger had to do to get on the front cover of *Rolling Stone* magazine. I told him you had to die first.

Sometimes when I walk on stage to perform, I start talking about all other artists I've known over the years. I say, 'I know more people dead than I know living.' I say, 'I think about Marvin Gaye, I think about Otis Redding, I think about Janis Joplin, I think about Jimi Hendrix. You don't know how fast these people can live their lives and go out so quick. They contribute so much in a short time.'

Ike Turner had a studio, Bolic Sound, down in Inglewood. It had an underground passageway that ran from the studio to his apartment.

There was a kitchen, a place to shoot pool, three studios. He had this place tricked out with cameras and mirrors. They were everywhere and that just added to the paranoia.

He had bars on the windows and push buttons on the doors, which locked everyone in. And Ike liked locking people in and not letting them out. He was a kid with a lot of toys.

There was also cocaine. Intimidation, humiliation, threats. There was always people hanging, a lot of people around all the time, up for seven-day weekends and Ike would go to sleep in the middle of it all. That, or he would be up raving. Ranting, raving and shouting. And issuing challenges.

But Ike was very talented. He knew how to put a band together, he knew the music side, wrote songs. And he got some big names down on tape at Bolic. I recorded there. And Marvin Gaye, Stevie Wonder, the Rolling Stones. What happened to the tapes? Ask Ike. Ike called and said, 'If you come to my studio, you don't have to go through that bullshit. You can get right on the board, you can work, I'll give you half the price that other studios would cost you.' But then you had to be locked in.

Sometimes, somebody would get to go out and a whole load of people would run out with them.

Ike and his wife Tina had opened for the Rolling Stones on their American tours in 1966 and 1969. One time when the Stones came in to town they went down to check Ike out, see his layout – this was during the early 1970s drug days; a gram of coke would never do, it was always two or three ounces in a big bowl on the console. Also, no one could have told the Stones that they didn't want to go down to Ike's place, not unless they wanted to be there for a week.

Ike locked them in. He had the Stones' management outside banging on the door, Mick and Keith trying to pull the bars off the windows. Still he wouldn't let them out. Ike had the Stones scared.

We all got more paranoid and devious and fucked up down at Bolic. Ike caught a friend of mine stealing blow one time. It turned ugly quick.

Another time I was down there with my wife and she was pregnant. She couldn't stay up all night and morning and I told Ike we had to go.

'OK, Bobby,' he said. 'I'll drive you. I'll get the car.'

He drove us, but without lights. He made a bet. He said, 'I can get to your house in 15 minutes.'

I said, 'I know you can, but just take your time.'

'No. I'm going to show you how fast I can get there.'

Ike cut off his lights, put his foot on the gas and the needle started climbing. We were crossing junctions, moving at 70, 75, 80, 85mph up through Inglewood, hitting La Cienega north at 90mph. The car jumped up and down, hit a dip, screeched around a corner. I said – I *screamed* – 'Man, she'll have this baby in the fucking car.'

It was a miracle we never got stopped by the cops. Madness. Him and Sly Stone were both crazy like that.

I once told Ike I was in pretty good condition, that I used to run a lot. He thought that was weird. No surprise there. I told him I could run ten miles and there was no way he could keep up with me. That was all the challenge he needed.

He turned off the mixing desk, told a drudge, 'Get me

169

a sweatsuit, get me some running shoes, sweat bands.' He got himself kitted out pretty good, but we weren't halfway around the block when I knew he was in trouble. He started panting hard, then he leaned against a wall to catch his breath. We were back inside Bolic inside of five minutes and he never mentioned running again. He told me, 'Man, you are in shape.'

Tina wouldn't be around so much, unless she was in the studio doing vocals. And come the night – and next morning – she was always in bed. She did the right thing, stayed away, and I think Ike wanted it that way. Whenever I saw her, she was always very humble, asked how we got on in the studio.

A guy called Bob Krasnow had a record company called Blue Thumb. Krasnow had travelled the country with James Brown and ran King Records in San Francisco, then Karma Sutra in LA. Krasnow hooked up with former A&M producer Tommy LiPuma and created Blue Thumb. Captain Beefheart came up with the name.

This was 1971 and I was hot. And what do people do when you're hot? They hook you up with someone else.

I went down to the Blue Thumb offices on North Canon Drive in Beverly Hills and they paired me up with Szabo and told me to give him some of my songs. So I did.

Gabor was a real sweetheart of a guy, a Hungarian who'd been around since the 1960s playing jazz. Had his own little sextets and quintets, but he was fucked on heroin. Lot of talent, but mad on smack.

170

I had taken a big advance from Blue Thumb so they called a lot, trying to catch me. They wanted to know when I had some songs for Gabor. Tomorrow, I told them. They would try me the next day and I told them the same thing. 'Nearly ready, I got five songs; give me a couple more days.' I had nothing.

Then Gabor would ask. I told him what I had told LiPuma, said I'd be ready for the studio the next week.

Finally, I got a call. There were to be no more excuses. They wanted me in the studio right away. I said, 'Fine, I was just about to call you. I got all the material.' I didn't have one song.

We got in the studio. I was playing rhythm guitar and started playing melodies. Gabor asked me what it was. I told him. Gave him some title. 'Just A Little Communication' was 'Bobby's Tune #1'.

So I would do another, duh duh duh da da. They asked what was that? Told them 'Bobby's Tune'. So 'If You Don't Want My Love' was 'Bobby's Tune #2', 'Fingers' was 'Gabor's Womack', 'Amazon' was 'Bobby's Tune #3', 'Azure Blue' was 'Bobby's Tune #4' and 'Breezin'' was 'Sister Sonorita'. Gave him four songs in total and a lot of melodies.

I took all these guys on a trip. Told the bassist what to play and the guy on keyboards. I just made it up. Afterwards, they apologised and said, 'We thought you were just bullshitting.'

'Breezin'' was the thing that caught the eye real fast. Everyone thought it would be a classic. I laughed. I had just made it up.

Five years later, George Benson called me. He wanted to cover 'Breezin''. He wanted me to play rhythm on his version. He thought I was the only one who could play that rhythm pattern. I said I'd have to think about it. I thought, 'Jazz artists, they don't sell a lot of records.'

I figured they could get someone else to do it. I made all kinds of excuses. Benson kept calling. I told him I would go down to help out, but wouldn't show. I sat at the house doing absolutely nothing.

I must have got tired of saying no. One time he called, I said yes. That time I showed. I laid down the track and George Benson played the lead. Next thing he's got a hit song. I had to pay $350 to get a copy of the platinum album. I guess they were mad at having to chase me around.

CHAPTER 13

THERE'S A RIOT GOIN' ON

Jim Ford, my writing partner, had a good idea. He came over to my place and told me that I needed to 'get something going – away from everything else that was going on'. He meant all the friction I had in my life.

I didn't know it, but the friction was just about to be turned up – to way past full blast. Jim wanted to hook me up with Sly Stone.

Sly had got his shit together in '67 when he created the Family Stone. There was Sly's brother Freddie, his sister Rose, Larry Graham on bass, Greg Errico on drums and a couple on horns – Cynthia Robinson and Jerry Martini.

They'd been cooking some dope-fuelled shit for a while and that was why Jim thought Sly might be good for me. He knew I needed a little comfort. It was the beginning of a weird period. I was still young, but really didn't know who I was. I had just fallen from a crazy marriage, and I was about to get into some more crazy shit.

I thought I was close to burning out as a man. The plan was to be around another musician my age. Someone I could work with and be inspired by. Get back into the music. Plus, Sly was a Pisces, same as me.

So I stumbled in there with Sly. For a while, I could forget the whole fucking world, forget who I was, where I was and what I was. I didn't know how long it would last or that it would be one of the greatest experiences of my life. In the end, it lasted too long.

Sly was crazy. Jim knew it, that's why he warned me. 'Look, Bobby,' he said. 'I want you to meet Sly, but you got to promise me one thing: you'll never go over his place without me.'

Me and Sly met for the first time at an Italian place. We got cosy in a couple of booths right at the back of the joint. Sly in one, me in the other. He turned around and asked, 'You Bobby Womack?'

'Yeah, man. And you're Sly.'

I was still trying to fill Sam's shoes, to act the businessman like him. So I was kitted out in a suit and loafers and sporting a briefcase. Sly didn't dig it. He told me, 'Hey, you're Bobby Womack. You're too funky to have a briefcase. Take that goddamn suit off and give me that fucking briefcase. You ain't got nothing in there anyway.' It was true, nothing but my sandwiches and a blueberry muffin for lunch.

I found out early on that Sly was two people. First, there was Sylvester Stewart, who was pretty cool, generous, creative, a genius musician. Then there was Sly

174

Stone. He was the destructive character. Sly was the kind of guy who liked to start fights just to see people go crazy and get tripped out. I was the guy who liked to put the fire out, make everybody cool.

We were alike in that we were so whacked out together, both like fish out water trying to survive. I thought Sly could help me get off being down on myself and help me just get on with life.

We also had pretty similar backgrounds, me and Sly. He was out of San Francisco, sang a lot of gospel songs 'cos like me he was from the sanctified and holiness school. Holy Lordy churches where they shout and cry and dance and then they're happy.

Sly was always in church. His old man was a preacher, his old lady an evangelist. Church, church, church.

But Sly was the little black sheep of the family who broke loose and, when he started to do something else, it wasn't nothing like church. He became a DJ in Oakland. The story went that he had a piano in the studio and when he gave a record a spin he would play along on the keyboard. Sly would improvise a new opening, middle or end. He'd tell his audience, 'Man, this could have been a hit record if only the guy hadn't let it go flat right there.' Then he'd add his little tune to liven things up. People would call in to ask him to do his versions.

Despite Jim Ford's warning, I practically moved into Sly's house in Bel Air 'cos I knew it was a place I could hang. As soon as I got over there, Sly said, 'Hey, you're a

175

bad nigger, you're a bad motherfucker, here have some coke.' He was going to be my hope-to-die partner.

It was a ride going on in that house; used to be where The Mamas and The Papas bunked. He had two big peacocks out there at the front, sort of like the first line of security, but the guards in that place were controlling devils and I knew you needed Jesus on your side to be with Sly Stone.

Everything was locked up and no one left until it was time to leave – and that was when Sly decided. There were a lot of drugs around and sometimes it seemed like everyone in LA was staying up there in Sly's house. He'd stay up six, seven days with the drugs, and with that kind of punishment you are going to hallucinate. We did that a lot of times. I stayed up maybe three or four days; I was the kind of guy who always said, 'I got to go to bed.'

We became very close very quickly because we had our music together. The music was unreal and we made a ton of it together. I worked on Sly's 1971 album *There's A Riot Goin' On*, playing guitar.

Sly liked the way I played, told me to play what I felt, which was a good vibe and that was the most fun you can ever have with music. I played wah-wah all over that album and Sly just ran tapes the whole time, capturing the sound. When you're singing and you're out there like that, you knew it would happen. It would come out sometime; I just had to trust it and let it happen

Sly's home studio was a good place for me to hang my head while the music was on. Everybody in the house was high on weed and coke and we would stay up night after night and play. Play, play some more and then play it again. One time Sly finally did get some sleep – on top of his piano. That's where I found him around five one morning. When I woke him gently, he looked up and started singing, 'One child grows up to be somebody that just loves to learn and another child grows up to be somebody you'd just love to burn...' It was from 'Family Affair'.

Sly taught me a lot about freedom, in music and life. I was also pretty impressed with Sly. I thought his music was superb, the best, man. He never wrote love songs and thought I was a dreamer because I did. He told me, 'You always write the wrong songs, crying like a baby, always crying. No bitch is going to make me cry.' Maybe our background wasn't so similar. 'You from a different church, brother,' he said. 'You just want to believe there is a Santa Claus.'

Maybe, but I told him that his songs were just about getting high. 'That's all you write.'

'Yeah, because that's what I do,' he reasoned. 'That's real. Real people who get high and come out bad.'

We played a lot together and recorded a lot too. The song 'When The Weekend Comes' was something that came out when we worked. I was always looking for the weekend. People party then because they got to work Monday through Friday, but come Friday they can get to hang out, spend their money, get drunk, whatever their release. We were fortunate because we got to party every night.

Sly and me, we also toured together, although that was always a mess because there would be about 30 people all dressed in costume, some of them trying to pitch for the job I was doing. Sly would spot a guy dressed like Snow White and he'd want him in the band. Didn't matter the guy couldn't play guitar, Sly loved the attire. I'm playing in the band and there's a guy behind me dressed like a cartoon character.

Someone needed to rein that shit in, but it wasn't going to be Sly. There was always some kind of problem. Sly acted strange in hotels. He would always have an enormous entourage: his goons, then everyone else, including the guy in the Show White outfit.

He would get in his room and then take everyone's keys, tell his security that no one could eat until he did. You weren't even supposed to make a phone call. It was like being in the army.

In New York once I was playing bass – Sly's bass player had left; his band was always leaving. Sly was out of funds to pay the hotel bill, which was stacked pretty high, around ten grand, because there was something like 20 rooms to take care of.

Sly was stranded; I was stranded. We were all stranded, hadn't eaten for something like three days, and the hotel was on our ass. I offered to call Pickett, see if old Wicked would bail us all out. Wilson Pickett was no fan of Sly's; he'd told me to leave him alone before my career got ruined.

But this was a jam. 'Pickett, I'll pay you back when I get back home,' I promised. 'Sly just needs $10,000.'

So Pickett called by with the cash and handed it to Sly. Sly – I don't know why he wanted to create a problem because Pickett already didn't like him – snatched the money out of his hand and snapped, 'You fucker, you should have been here with that 15 minutes ago.'

But Sly could come through good and did. I was in trouble myself with a gig. It was at the Greek Theater in LA. The O'Jays opened up, but before that my band – and it was a big one, a 12-piece – demanded a pay rise. I guess they figured they would stick that right on me before the gig so I would be forced to cough up the extra. I told them I would sing a cappella before that happened, fired them and then sat up all night trying to put together another bunch of musicians.

I got a drummer, but didn't know he was tripped out on acid. I was in trouble. To make it worse, I fell going on stage. I was wearing a long cape and it caught in my heels. It was going to be a thin show, me and no musicians.

Then I looked back and Sly's band filed on, one by one. Sly had found out about my band problem and sent over his guys, who had my shit down. Sly told them to get up on stage with me and do their thing. And they did, they walked out and bailed me and the show out.

Another time Sly and me were riding in a limo together. The driver was an Arab. Black suit, black peaked cap, the whole chauffeur thing down. He kept stealing glances at us through the rear view. What he saw through that mirror: someone with very long hair or a wig, big shades, boots halfway up his leg, fur hat, probably two hats.

The driver couldn't tell if it was a man or a woman. And a guy with him – me – snorting something up his nostril.

I felt a little sick because I'd also been taking some pills and had washed them down with some booze. Sly tapped on the glass separating us and the driver, and ordered him to pull over before I puked all over the leather seats and oriental rug-style carpeting, but the chauffeur refused, and told us I would have to hold it in until we reached the next gas station. I couldn't wait that long. I started throwing up and the chauffeur had a fit.

Didn't bother Sly. When the guy finally got around to pulling over, Sly got out and chased the man across the highway, a ten-lane freeway. Picture that, Sly chased the guy with all that shit on it. Both of them could have ended up getting killed. Sly got back in the car, this time in the driver's seat. He took off, leaving the chauffeur stood by the side of the road.

Sometimes when I stayed with Sly out on the road, he would have a private jet laid on, but the plane never got off the ground. We'd sit there getting high and he would tell the pilot that we weren't ready to go.

Pilot: 'But, Mr Stone, you have spent $8000 since you've been sitting here all this time.'

Sly: 'We're just about to go. What kind of food you got on this jet?'

Pilot: 'We got nuts.'

Sly: 'That's no good. We got to go to a restaurant.'

That was another $8000 burned by a plane standing on a runway for four or five hours.

Sly's gig philosophy was not my philosophy. I always had that professionalism drilled into me by my father and Sam that, when it's time to work, get on and hit it.

Sly didn't run by that book. He sat there many times before a show and told me he couldn't do it. 'I can't go, man,' he'd tell me.

I didn't understand, but I asked why.

'It's hard enough for me to talk, let alone stand up and try to sing,' he said.

His problem was he couldn't wait until the gig was over before doing the drugs. He didn't mess with nothing but cocaine, but when he found out you could cook it he became a chef.

Sly said, 'It's hard to wait, I just do a little bit and then I'm going out on stage.'

He tried to turn me on to his way of thinking too, said it was expected in our line of work. He thought I was too square; he said, 'Bobby, if The Man told you to turn up at 9pm, you would be there at 8.30pm, but let me tell you a little something about showbusiness: it don't work like that. It's what you don't do that gives you mystique. Don't be available all the time, don't always be there.'

Many times, he said, 'I can't walk out there.' He meant the stage.

I couldn't understand that. 'You came all the way out here with this whole band,' I reasoned, 'everybody is waiting on you and you are sitting looking out the window watching the people walk in.'

He would watch and laugh at some of the straight dudes

181

lined up with their dates, pointing out their unhip gear. Man, it was like he hoped they hadn't bought tickets to come and see him. Who did he think they had come for?

The funny thing was, Sly was actually convinced he never missed a gig, nor was even late for one. 'Bobby,' he told me, 'see what happened? The people got there before I left. So they have to wait.' It made no sense. He would still be backstage and I'd tell him, 'Sly, they've been waiting for hours.'

'But I ain't missed the gig.'

He got high and it made him paranoid, and that's when I knew. First, it was cool, then it got to be too much. You can't do all the drugs and go out in front of an audience. It's a serious thing when you walk out on stage. Music is spiritual and an audience can tell if you've started tripping before they have.

I thought it was a blessing for an artist to be able to entertain, to be given that gift, so I thought he should respect his art form. I didn't want to go on stage fucked up; I was out there to sing. After, that's a different matter. That was my time, on my own, at home and I could do what I wanted with it. I realised I could not put drugs in my system and then go on stage and try and reach God. It just don't work.

But I liked coke. So, shit, I got high after I came off stage. That was the way it worked. I had some kind of system, I didn't get high before an interview or a gig, but when that ended the night was mine. Again, Sly didn't subscribe to that philosophy. He said, 'Fuck that shit.'

Weird shit went down in that house too. Sly had a dog called Gun, a vicious pitbull terrier. Fierce fucker. There was also a little monkey knocking around the house and the monkey would tease Gun rotten. The dog could never catch it and it would drive him wild, always snapping.

Sly would encourage the monkey to fuck with the pitbull. Gun would charge after the monkey, but the chimp was too quick and he'd jump right back up a tree or on a fence. This went on for ages

The pitbull must have thought there was some way to end it. Sure enough, one day the monkey jumped down and went 'heh, heh, heh' to get Gun's attention but, when he went to run and jump back out of the way, his foot slipped. Man, that was it. Gun was on it like lightning. First thing he did was bite a hole in the monkey's chest, then turned the chimp over and fucked it. That dog was vicious.

Sly would get wired sometimes and walk through the house with Gun. He'd shout for us to find a place to hide out. 'Everybody hit the deck, the man is coming looking for you,' he'd announce.

I ran into a room looking for a place to hide. Nothing, just a pool table. I could hear Sly calling out and that vicious dog of his straining at his leash, but I thought that dog could pull skinny old Sly over real easy, then I'd be dead before he got back off the ground.

I pushed the pool balls in the pockets and clambered up on that table and held my breath. I could hear my heart pounding as I pressed myself close to that green baize. The door opened and I heard Gun pant. He trotted in, tugging Sly behind on that lead. I squeezed my eyes tight shut and wished I could fit in one of the ball pockets.

I listened as the pair of them did a circuit of the pool table with me laid out on top of it.

'Nothing here, boy,' said Sly.

Then, just as they headed for the door again, Sly leaned over and whispered close so the dog couldn't hear: 'Bobby, ain't no problem for Gun to jump up on that pool table. You'd better get yourself a better hidey hole next time, bro.'

Sly had a little gangsta thing going on. I don't know why, because Sly was definitely no tough guy. There were always guns lying around and he would get his goons – one time it was a family out of New York, huge guys, really tough headcrackers – to fight each other to prove who was the meanest son of a bitch.

Everybody was testing somebody. I saw some guys get their asses whupped real bad. And if you walk with that crowd you always bring violent people to the door. Drugs would be stolen. A guy might come back with his crew and then there'd be a fight. A lot of that stuff went on.

That's when the music began to take a back seat. I started to see all the bad shit go into the music. It was scary. When we made music it wasn't happy any more, it had a dark side to it. The girls and the gear had taken a front seat. And the gangstas? They were sitting right there next to them in the passenger seat. I saw things slowly falling apart.

Then Sly went to jail. Busted. I reached out for him and whenever he went to jail I went and got him out. I'd fight for him. It was the needy helping the needy because that's what they do.

I heard he got a doctor or psychologist to cop for him while he was doing time. Sly's method was to challenge the guy, tell the doc that he would never be able to understand a guy like Sly unless he'd gone through some of the same stuff – and that meant taking the same drugs. 'How can you talk to me about drugs?' he was supposed to have asked. 'You never saw a drug in your life. If you knew you'd try it.' He demanded to be treated by someone he could relate to.

Before long, he had the doc under the desk doing a rock and Sly dished out the therapy. The doctor also switched testing bottles so that nothing showed up in Sly's piss when it came around to screening for pharmaceuticals.

I knew I couldn't be around Sly much longer. And he wasn't the kind of guy you'd drop in on for half an hour and a cup of tea. The drugs had sheltered all my weaknesses, but I gradually started to break away from that scene and get my system clean. I got back into going to the studio, retreated into my music and worked on getting a new album out. The more I cleaned up my diet, the stronger I got.

It was a crazy story, but it wasn't one with a good ending. I was glad it was over and glad that whoever survived it survived. There weren't that many. A few came

185

out healthy or came out with their life or just came out, but a lot of people died or got hurt and some might be better off dead because they got so whacked out they didn't know who they were. A lot of casualties.

Sly's life was such a trip, but if he watched over all of that he might have wished he could have done things different. Because, if anyone made people focus on the whole drug scene, it was Sly. All the great music that he created, and he became known for his drug habit.

The last time I heard from Sly, he had gotten himself straight. I was riding down Hollywood Boulevard, minding my business, looking straight ahead. I made a stop at a red light and glanced over. There was Sylvester Stewart sat in a Ferrari staring over at me. I said, 'Hey, Sly.'

He said, 'Hello,' put his foot on the gas and drove off.

'Man,' I thought, as I watched his ride cruise off, 'what was that shit about?' All the stuff we had been through and everything.

Next thing, he backed up, leaned out the window and said, 'Hey, Bobby, sorry, man. I can't do that to you. How you doin', man?' Then he said, 'Call me.'

In 1970, Minit Records was absorbed into its parent group, Liberty, which closed a year later. Me and the rest of the roster were bumped over to United Artists.

This was a breakthrough. I was given the freedom to produce my own work and brought out *Communication* in 1971. It was a mix of covers – James Taylor's 'Fire And Rain', Ray Stevens's 'Everything Is Beautiful', a take on the Carpenters' '(They Long To Be) Close To You' – and some of my own tunes.

The biggest hit was the ballad 'That's The Way I Feel About Cha', which cracked the Top 30 and reached No 2 on the R&B charts early in 1972. All the time this was going on, I was helping Sly out on *There's A Riot Goin' On*.

I followed *Communication* with *Understanding* in 1972, recorded in a few feverish days at American Sound Studio in Memphis and Muscle Shoals, Alabama. One of the key songs was 'I Can Understand It', but they didn't put that out as a single. What they did release from *Understanding* was 'Woman's Gotta Have It', which I co-wrote with Barbara's daughter Linda.

'Woman's Gotta Have It' was an important song to me. Stuck through my whole life. I wanted to let men know that women are around for more than entertainment purposes. A woman has got to know that she is needed; she's got to know she ain't living or walking on shaky ground.

But I also wanted to say something to women at the same time. About respect. Coming from Squaresville, I could not understand hookers. I used to stop them on the street and ask them whether, if they had a good job, they would still hook. They told me it was their living and they didn't see a way out.

After a time I stopped. Those pimps would ask me, 'Man, what planet you come from? These bitches like to do that because they supposed to be like that.'

When I was on the road with Sam, I saw a lot of stuff. I guess I was too young to understand it all and, even if did know what was going on, that don't mean I accepted it. If I saw a woman going in one of the musicians' rooms, I'd tell her he'd had another woman in there not half an hour before, said things like, 'He don't love you. They just want to get you drunk and run a train on you.'

So she would go in and tell him and he'd come out mad at me, ranting, 'He's a square, a young kid. He's just like that – saying those things – 'cos he can't get no pussy.' Then he might have said, 'Hey, man, keep your little mouth shut, if you can't say nothing about me good, don't say nothing at all. Fuck it, this is the game. This is what it is.'

So every night we would go to a different city and run the same game on different ladies. I didn't understand it and didn't want a woman like that. I wanted a wholesome woman, a clean woman; I wanted to make her the queen that she was.

With 'Woman's Gotta Have It', I laid it out, said if you really want to call yourself a man then you should treat a woman with respect. Treat her like you would your own mom.

A few years later, a famous rapper came to me. Instead of singing 'a woman's gotta have it', he wanted me to sing 'bitch ain't gonna have shit'. I told him I couldn't do it. He said, 'Bobby, it'll put another $175,000 in your pocket. Cash money.'

I said, 'Man, I still can't do it. First of all, my mom will

188

have to be dead and gone and she's very much alive. Then I really do believe if you got a woman and if you want a queen you got to behave like a king. It's as simple as that.' Also, I told him I couldn't go against what I'd sung in the 1970s; it would have been like I hadn't really believed what I said.

We recorded 'Woman's Gotta Have It' at American Sound and it became my first No 1 R&B hit, topping the charts in the spring of 1972.

As the follow-up, UA released my cover of Neil Diamond's 1969 hit 'Sweet Caroline (Good Times Never Seemed So Good)'. That did OK, but a lot of black jocks played the flip side 'Harry Hippie', the song about my brother, and that made No 8 on the R&B charts early in 1973.

Blaxpoitation movies were big in the early 1970s. Richard Roundtree was Shaft. I wanted UA to give me a movie soundtrack to do. I'd got two successful albums under my belt and for some reason I wanted to write a film score. I thought I would be moving up with that.

UA were reluctant, but eventually they conceded, told me they had the right film. It was called *Across 110th Street*, like in New York. Cross that street and you're in Harlem, the ghetto, not far from the Apollo where The Valentinos played with James Brown. Perfect, that was my territory. I had come from a ghetto so it was something I knew about. I knew all its stories.

Like this one: the ghetto kids don't know who I am, but their moms might. That fact once saved my life.

189

I went out to get some cash. I pulled over at a Bank of America on Ventura Boulevard, and stepped out. I was looking fine, got my velvet wide brim, pair of big old shades and a funky wool coat with a trim. I pulled my wallet out of my pocket, flashed my Amex card and stuck it in the cash machine in the wall. As soon as I'd done that, two guys walked up right behind me. One said, 'Don't look back or I'll blow your brains out, motherfucker.' He poked a gun into the small of my back.

I said, 'Hey, bro.'

He said, 'I ain't your brother.'

The guy with the gun pushed me to the parking lot behind the bank, the pistol pressing hard in my spine. I thought that was it. I was going to end up dead. Then I thought, 'That's the way it is, OK, that's it.'

Behind the bank, the guy with the gun snatched my hat off. Fuck it, it was only a hat. Then the guy told me to turn and give him my coat. He put the gun up to my head, pressed it against my right temple. I felt the barrel, cold and hard. A cold numbness spread from it, over me. It was weird, and hard to explain. All the good things in my life ran through my mind; it made me think life was beautiful.

I had my hands up, but I turned around slowly. Unbuttoned my coat, slipped it off and handed it over. Soon as I'd done that, the other cat – the guy watching nervously left and right – took a proper look at me for the first time. Then he said, 'Man, that's Bobby Womack.' He recognised me even with my shades on.

The guy with the gun looked around at him. The cat goes, 'Womack, the singer.'

The stick-up man just stared.

'I can't do it, man. I can't do it. My mother loves this motherfucker.'

The guy with the gun looked back at me.

The lookout said, 'Man, I'm off. I couldn't face my mother again.' He turned and ran off.

'Bobby Womack?' asked the gunman. I nodded. Then he shrugged and took off after him.

I stood there for a minute, tried to stop shaking. I picked up my hat lying on the ground, put it back on and walked away. That freaked me out, but at the point when he pressed the automatic to my head I was ready to go.

I wanted to see a movie dealing with stuff like that, and I thought I could write a million songs about it. I got taken to the movies to watch the picture and walked out with the film in my head, maybe not every plot twist but at least the vague concept − trying to survive in the ghetto.

Outside on the sidewalk, an executive told me I had two weeks to complete it, just 14 short days to finish the score. That's enough time to write a shopping list, a letter to your mom, maybe even a hit single, but a movie score? The other problem was that I had a long tour scheduled, so I was out on the road doing shows every night.

I worked it by writing every spare minute of the day; between gigs, between bus stops, on the plane, backstage, in my hotel. Writing, writing, writing, but not between sleep. I didn't sleep. Didn't have time.

When I finished writing, I gathered the musicians – my back-up band Peace – between sets to cut the material in a studio. I brought the masters back to UA. They were surprised I'd remembered the film, let alone written a soundtrack to go with it.

It was like my story. Written from the heart. The title track became my fifth straight Top 20 R&B hit in less than two years. It turned out to be a masterpiece, but typically I had to work under the worst possible conditions. It was like I couldn't use no pen or paper, no time to think, but I did it anyway.

A couple of decades later, Quentin Tarantino used the tune as the title track to his 1997 film *Jackie Brown*. That was kind of like a reunion because Pam Grier, who played Jackie, was an old girlfriend of mine and the cousin of one of my best buddies, Rosie Grier, the former all-pro defensive linesman for the LA Rams.

I turned back to The Valentinos for my next record. I dug out our 1962 hit 'Lookin' For A Love' for the next album, *Lookin' For Love Again*, and put it out as a single, which topped the charts for several weeks in spring 1974. Another single from *Lookin' for Love Again*, 'You're Welcome, Stop On By', reached No 5 on the R&B charts that summer.

In 1974, I also had to face another tragedy: the death of my brother Harry, the second youngest. We were born a year apart and were close, probably the closest brother I had. He was also the Harry in my song 'Harry Hippie'. I never really did find out if he liked that song.

Harry came to stay with me one Friday and was dead by the following Monday.

We were very different. As kids, we would imagine our futures, what we wanted to be, what we wanted to do. Harry's ambition was to live on a reservation with the Native Americans. He would have loved that. He watched Westerns all the time, even when he'd grown up he was still pushing to go live in some wilderness.

'You want people to toss you food from a plane?' I said, laughing at the thought of Harry in a tepee.

He said, 'They're free, man, they don't have to deal with a lot of stuff. Free spirits.'

Now, my map was simple, too, but it didn't involve cowboys and Indians. It was: get famous, move to Hollywood and get a big old mansion. Harry, he always laughed at that. I wasn't the sharpest tool in the box, I was slow at school, and Harry teased me, 'Oh, Bobby will be nothing but a janitor. That's what he's going to be.'

'We'll see.'

We went back and forth with that.

Harry never got it, why I would want to cut all those records. He knew what came with it. 'You get people on your case, you got to constantly come up and show them you still got it,' he said. 'Who wants to be under that kind of pressure? I feel sorry for you. I see you with all these people, this person doing that for you, another doing this, but these people don't care about you.'

He was right about that.

'All I need is my sandals, my jacket, my little pouch and some nice herb.' That was Harry, a hippy, a beatnik, a free spirit.

So when Jim Ford, one of my writing partners, brought a song to me about a free spirit I thought the story seemed to be about my brother. Jim hadn't written with Harry in mind so I rewrote it, putting my brother into the story.

Of course, by the time we had grown up, Harry wasn't on a reservation and he wasn't happy. He was always being compared with me. He was hearing that I was leaving him behind. 'You could be doing that,' people told him. We had both been Valentinos so it wasn't too hard to imagine. He would shrug and roll another joint, but maybe all the comparing and criticism got to him and was what broke him up.

I had started to make a bit of money, but got lost along the way. That meant I lost contact with all my brothers, including Harry, but one day in 1974 Harry called up. He told me he was having problems with his old lady. They were fighting like cats and dogs. He complained he was going crazy with it all.

He said, 'I need to get out of here, Bobby.'

'Why don't you come up to my house, stay with me,' I suggested.

So Harry came to stay. I was living up in the Hollywood Hills, at Firenze Place, off Mulholland Drive. I could go back to looking after my little brother. It seemed like he had lost contact with the world. He'd stumble around because he couldn't see too good, and he told me he needed glasses. I promised to fix him up with a pair.

By then he'd started using smack – snorting, not shooting – and also selling a few bags on the side to make himself some sort of living. When I saw the state he was in, the clothes he was wearing, I couldn't believe how far the two of us had drifted apart.

What made it worse seeing Harry down on his luck was I felt bad about myself, playing over what Sam had told me about not leaving my brothers. Thinking about when we used to sing together, me, Harry, Curtis and Cecil, and what would have come of Harry if we had stuck together as The Valentinos.

My girlfriend at the time, now she was a girl. The girl who put the voodoo on me. Part of this meant cutting pieces of my hair. I don't know why, maybe it was part of the ritual. She asked if I'd ever been to New Orleans – more hoodoo voodoo. I told her I'd never go there with her. I was going bald with all the hair cutting.

We were together five years. She was jealous. Man, that's right. She accused me of being with anyone.

Harry couldn't get a fix on that. He thought with me living up in my big house with money, with cars, with whatever, that things would be cool. But my girl didn't seem to think so.

One day he spilled out his thoughts. He said, 'Man, I thought you'd be happy here and your girlfriend would be happy. You got everything. I'm living down there, I ain't got nothing. People is saying, "Look at your brother, your brother has got this and that. What are you doing with your life, Harry?' But the way I see it, there ain't no difference. We both got our problems, Bobby. The only difference is yours are bigger, they get noticed a little more and it costs a little more.'

He was in a bad space. It was like we knew his time was running out. He even said that he believed one of us was going to be killed and he wanted it to be him. He figured I would have a better chance at looking after the rest of the family and Mom and Dad.

That was sad. I told him not to talk like that and we'd both work out fine, but he knew there was a higher power working behind the scenes. I wanted to get him out in the world again and take his mind off his problems so I gave him a car and sorted those glasses so he had no excuse about driving it.

As he drove away from the house, he shouted out that he didn't want to go on his own. 'Do you want a ride?'

'No, man, you've got to do this on your own. You've got to get back into the real world.'

He said, 'I know you love me, man.'

As he hit the gas pedal, I thought I could get him to come back and play bass with me, get us working together again, just like in The Valentinos.

'Where shall I go?'

'Anywhere, man. Just get lost, anywhere you want to go, you're a free man now.'

A couple of hours later, I got a call. He was lost. 'How

196

do you get back up into those hills?' he asked. He was down on himself for not being able to do that one thing and also to take care of himself.

'Hey, don't worry about it,' I told him. 'It's not like you're going to a meeting.' I gave him some directions.

'OK,' he said.

Three hours later, I got another call. He was still lost, still trying to get back up into the Hollywood Hills. He'd filled the car up twice with gas he'd done so much driving.

I had a gig up in Seattle and I told Harry that when I got back he should pick up the bass again and we'd go into rehearsal. I flew up to Seattle with my girlfriend. She made the night hell. If the maid came into my room, she'd accuse me of sleeping with her. We had a big fight, a real screamer, and I ended up putting her out of my hotel suite because I couldn't take it any more.

That night I went out on the prowl. I thought, 'Fuck it, I'm getting grief for not fucking anyone, I might as well pick a chick up.' Typical of my luck, there weren't any hot ladies hanging about the club I played, but there was a hooker, a white prostitute. She told me it was a hundred bucks – not much more than the whore in New York when The Valentinos played the Apollo.

Then I had a change of plan. I figured I could just fuck with my girlfriend's head a bit. I told the hooker that I only wanted her to come back to my hotel and act like we'd known each other a long time.

The hooker played ball. 'Whatever your kicks are, honey.'

Back at the hotel, I saw the light under the door of my girl's room and I made sure she could hear us walk down the corridor. As we waltzed past her room – me saying, 'Baby, I'm so glad I met you, this is going to be fun. You've got to stay over tonight' – I heard the door creak open.

Inside my suite, the hooker was a little surprised she'd already earned her money and kept her clothes on. 'What do you want to do?'

'No, that's it,' I told her.

'Really?'

'Yeah, but you can stay here if you want.'

I put her out on a couch, locked the doors and went to bed. 'Leave in the morning or whenever you want.'

I don't know how my girlfriend got in that suite; she must have gone through about four locked doors to get at that girl on the couch, but I was woken by screams and someone being hit.

Blood was all over the show. That was scary. My girlfriend was raving and she threatened, 'I could have killed you a long time ago, but I'm not going to hurt you. I'm going to kill her.'

On the floor, the hooker's coat lay in about five pieces, slashed by a knife. No one was going to be wearing that again.

I managed to get my girlfriend out of there, but before too long she was back knocking on the door to my suite again. I couldn't handle it. She was pleading to be let in again and then started going crazy on me – giving me more of her wild, crazy voodoo shit. And it was vile, evil.

She said, 'Bobby, please I got to talk you. I just had a dream I saw Harry in a casket.' That's what she said.

I couldn't believe it. Not after her trick with the whore. I said, 'Shut the fuck up talking like that.'

'I saw him in a casket, Bobby.'

I warned her to stop the crazy shit and that if I did open the door I would probably hurt her, but she kept at it telling me Harry was dressed in a white suit and lying in a coffin. 'Harry's dead,' she said.

I wouldn't answer her no more.

The next day I had a radio show to do. It was the kind of thing where I'd go on, shoot the breeze, take a few calls and drum up a bit of trade for the next show. I was at the station and the show's producer put through a call from my brother Cecil.

I was surprised, but ran with it. 'Hey, Cecil, what's up, man?'

He said, 'Harry got killed.'

Man, I freaked out.

The disc jockey cut the sound, the radio went dead, and I went nuts. I couldn't believe it. I sat there stunned. Not before too long – I don't know how many hours passed – Bill Withers showed up at the radio station and tried to console me. He'd heard Cecil and had driven over to support me.

A girlfriend of Harry's had gone up to my house to see him, took him up a bit of weed. She must have been looking through the closets because she found some women's clothes and got it into her head that Harry was fooling around. They were my girlfriend's clothes. Harry hadn't been fooling with anyone.

While Harry smoked a joint and kicked back watching TV, this woman snuck into my kitchen and got herself a steak knife – one of the ones I cooked with – from a drawer, walked back into the living room and plunged it into his neck.

The knife was still in his neck when the ambulance and cops arrived. Poor Harry couldn't take the knife out of his neck; I guess it was just hurting so bad, but he got up, walked around, opened the front door and went outside to sit on the porch where he bled to death.

Curtis was the first brother on the scene. He told me afterwards that when he turned up Harry had already lost a lot of blood but was still just about clinging on. As he lay dying, Curtis asked him to squeeze his hand if he could hear him. Harry squeezed. It was about the last thing he did.

What made it worse was a couple of neighbours had seen Harry sat out there on the porch, but didn't want to get involved. The doctors reckoned Harry might have made it if they had got to him earlier.

The funeral was just depressing, so sad. We had it at the cemetery at Forest Lawn, all us brothers dressed alike – suits and ties, the whole bit – just as we'd been on stage, but burying a younger brother was sad.

I started blaming my girlfriend for the whole thing. She'd been the first to tell me, but in my mind it was like she had put a jinx on him. She had to go.

On the back of Harry's death, I was too broke up to work, and the drugs and partying at Sly's place had all taken their toll. But I had a ton of dates I was committed to. Things were still steaming but mentally and physically I wasn't up for doing any gigs.

The problem was the promoters had already put up their money and I thought the whole thing was being billed around Harry's death. Roll up, roll up, come and hear Harry Hippie's brother. I wasn't going for that. That's when the blind thing came in.

I was sick, sad and depressed; I would have grabbed at anything. Then an idea came to fake a bad fall. I thought that might get me off some dates. I staged the whole thing at a recording studio, somewhere public. I fell back and pretended to hit the back of my head hard against the wall, then claimed that I couldn't see. I got myself to a hospital and the doctors did some tests. One of them was to strike a match real close to my eye to see if I flinched. I didn't.

The diagnosis was that it was some kind of psychological thing – a little temporary blindness brought on by the fall and all the pressure I was under following Harry's death. The medics thought that I would recover with some R&R.

It seemed like I'd hoodwinked the medical fraternity because they got my eyes all patched up, gave me a cane, the whole nine yards, but I still had to go through with a couple of dates.

What a charade. The first date, at Madison Square Garden in New York, I had my brother Friendly lead me out on stage, gauze and tape wrapped around my head. He was in on the ruse and introduced me to the audience. I asked him if he thought I could get away with it. He didn't see any alternative. 'It's going to have to work, bro.' He was right. I knew I'd be in a hell of a lot of trouble if I got caught out.

I had to be fucked out of my mind. I totally overdid the blind-man bit, stumbling around, knocking over the microphone, tripping over amps, spilling drinks, but a blind guy ain't that obvious. He doesn't 'act' blind. I'd worked with a few, Ray Charles and both sets of Blind Boys. I knew how they got by in a world without light and it wasn't like that.

One of the most embarrassing episodes of the whole embarrassing episode was that Stevie Wonder – himself blind almost since birth – got to hear about my blindness and came to wish me well. He tried to cheer me up, told me it wasn't the end of the world, and while he told me this I could peep out of the corner of my eye, behind all the gauze, and see Stevie sitting there sympathising.

I managed to slip out of a lot of those dates. United Artists advised me to take a break: drop the rest of the tour, get myself over to Hawaii and try and ditch the depression.

I called my old friend Gorgeous George O'Dell and he told me to take his wife, Cathy. She hadn't been to Hawaii and was a little bored. George also said I'd be doing him a favour because he couldn't afford to take his wife on a vacation like that. 'I trust you,' he said as an aside.

The thing was, George's old lady was fine. Very fine. I

mean, she was beautiful, definitely the gorgeous one of the pair. So I felt a little bad because my thoughts about the trip weren't all pure.

Cathy and me flew to out to the islands and I was the happiest (pretend blind) person in the whole world. There was a yacht laid on, and parties were thrown for me. It was a trip. What I didn't know was the president of the record company, Mike Stewart, had instructed some guy to follow me around and check I wasn't misbehaving.

One night, me and Cathy were sat up in our hotel suite drinking champagne. I'd managed to keep my whole act together, but a small piece of the cotton gauze around my head kept slipping into the corner of my eye. It was irritating so I was constantly pulling at it.

I did this one time while we sipped the bubbly and there was Cathy sat there doing her nails – naked. Not one stitch of clothing on. She must have slipped out of her dress while we were talking. I tried not to stare, but it was hard. Actually, it was impossible.

Cathy got up off the bed to dry her nails, shaking her wrists and waltzing around the room. I forgot I was supposed to be blind and my eyes and head followed her every movement.

Suddenly, she caught on to the way I was watching her. She shot me a look, realised I was as blind as she was. Then she screamed, 'Oh, my God, you bastard.' And she ran out to fetch a towel. 'Bobby, oh, Lord.' She screamed so hard, 'Bobby, how could you do something like this? I've got to get another room. You scared the shit out of me.'

I tried to calm her down, but felt like a fraud. I pleaded with her. I explained about the depression Harry's death had dropped me in, and how I couldn't face going on the road. 'I had to do it; I had no other way out.'

She got on the phone to George and told him I was faking my blindness. I could hear them. 'Yes, he can see... No, he's not blind... It's all a scam...'

It was so embarrassing. I told George the same I'd told his wife and tried to convince him that the blindness wasn't a plot to lure Cathy to Hawaii. And that, no, I hadn't touched her. 'It's the God's truth, it's all because of Harry,' I pleaded.

George was cool, and he told me to slow down, relax. So I ironed it out, at least with George and his wife, and we got on with the vacation.

However, Dr Shovac then got in on the act. He spotted us on the beach. That would have been OK, but at the time I was chasing down the sand and splashing through the surf. I'd tossed away my white stick and shed my bandages as I ran along the sand like the Invisible Man unwrapping his head.

The guy the record company had hired saw it all. He got on the blower to LA and reported in.

I'd been charging the whole trip to UA. Anything you want. Champagne? Oh, put it on the tab. Dinner? Charge it. A new outfit? The company will pay. Jewellery? Yeah, we got to have jewellery. We'd only been there a week and the bill was already around $30,000.

When we got back to the hotel after our frolic on the

204

beach, the hotel receptionist had a message for me from the label. It read something like: 'Mr Womack, all your funds have been cut off, there is a plane back to LA tonight. Get your butt on it.' Man, I'd been rumbled.

I tried arguing, but the hotel people said they were just doing their job and their job was to cut everything off and get me on the next plane out of there.

So that was it. We had to go home, and I had to face the music with the record company. I caught a lot of flak for pulling that stunt. The record company thought I was crazy and I had to turn the whole thing around without the press finding out or my career was over.

The plan was for me to claim I'd gone back into hospital and had been treated successfully, but some of the promoters on those cancelled gigs must have got wind of the whole shaky deal. A bunch of them clubbed together and threatened to sue me for breach of contract. They made it plain that if I ever set foot in their towns they would serve papers on me.

It got to the point where I was waiting for these promoters to die off so I could hit their towns and work again. I went out of the country to do dates, places like England, Germany, France and Italy, places where the promoters weren't out to ambush me with legal papers.

It was a while before I could get back into the States, several years before the problem really went away. I asked my manager, 'Hey, is Mr So-and-So still around?'

'He died.'

OK, that meant I could play Jackson.

'And what about Mr You-Know?'

'Yeah, he's still around. He's still promoting.'

Shit. That meant Reno was still off limits.

Finally, I did one show in Arizona and I was signing some autographs at a record store and one of the promoters was waiting in line. He obviously hadn't died. I tried to play it cool. I said, 'Hey, Willy. You get some free tickets and dinner is on me tonight.'

He must have got tired waiting to hit me with that writ because he never served it. He told me my luck was in and then had that dinner.

I had to get back to recording, but I had an idea about that, too. I wanted to cut a country and western album. United Artists didn't understand it. They didn't want it, either. Told me I wasn't a C&W singer. They thought I had been hanging with Sly too long.

I said, 'Well, that's the only album you're going to get. And I want all my brothers on it, too.'

At that point, I had a lot of ambitions. To do movie scores, play instrumentals, play jazz, a comedy album. I even had a crazy idea about opening up a barbeque restaurant on wheels, but no one wanted to back it.

In those days, record companies just wanted an artist to tread the same line. Their attitude was, if you were cutting hit songs, why change the formula? Keep with the hits and don't worry about nothing else.

I kept pressing with the C&W album. C&W was going to be big and I wanted in on the ground floor, was my reasoning. Finally, they gave me the green light. It was just crazy. My father came out to sing on it, had my brothers there too.

That was one thing I'd always wanted to do, to have my father on the record. It was the only time we got the whole family together, which was what was so spiritual about it. I thought *BW Goes C&W* was a great album, great songs. I really sung my heart out.

The cover shoot took a western theme. All us brothers dolled up in cowboy outfits. Guns, holsters, spurs, boots, the whole bit, but C&W meant nothing without horses and that meant us sitting on the damn things. None of us had been around horses, let alone ridden one, and, every time one of us finally got saddled up, the horse would take off, buck until we fell off and head back to the stable. I was running around that field trying to coral those horses.

I've got a picture in my mind of Friendly Jr, reins in his hand one minute, hanging upside down from the horse's belly the next. We finally tethered the horses to this post so they wouldn't buck, but it took a whole day for the photographer to wrap the shoot.

Then I told the label the name I had planned for the album: *Step Aside Charley Pride Give Another Nigger A Try*. The way I saw it was simple. Charley Pride was the only black man singing C&W and now there was another black man who wanted to give it a shot.

There was nothing spiritual in how the record company received that. They exploded. The president refused to put out an album with that kind of title.

Naturally, the – mostly white – suits at the label had a big problem with the word 'Nigger'.

'Why have you got to use the word nigger?' the execs asked.

'A brother can call another nigger a nigger,' I explained. 'You can't call him that, but I can because I'm one too.'

If all that wasn't bad enough, I was also getting grief from the western actor Gene Autry because I had used his song 'I'm Back In The Saddle Again', but corrupted the title to 'I'm Black In The Saddle Again'. The Singing Cowboy called me to complain. He told me the song was close to his heart and he wouldn't tolerate me using it the way I wanted. He took out a lawsuit and threatened to sue me to the end of the world if I used his song like that. The label, and everyone else, thought I was mocking him.

The label finally talked me out of the album title, told me they would never go for it and would fight me tooth and nail. Somebody came up with *BW Goes C&W* as in Bobby Womack goes Country & Western. Label president Mike Stewart asked, 'Is that going to kill you, Bobby?'

I reckoned not. 'OK, man, fuck it, you guys.'

The he told me, 'Oh, by the way, we're selling your contract.'

They thought I had finally flipped out.

I always look at *BW Goes C&W* as a classic piece of work. I wasn't trying to be funny. I felt I was on a roll, cooking, and when you're on a roll the road ahead can take you anywhere. I wanted to explore that new territory. I wanted to say what I found and say it the way my people would understand it, but that meant I was hurting my career. All I heard from labels was 'you can't write that' or 'the market won't go for it'. They always wanted me to shape things for the market and not to offend anyone. I didn't go with that.

The only hit I had in 1975 was 'Check It Out', with 'Daylight' coming a year later. *BW Goes C&W* was my last album for UA. They sold my contract to Columbia. On paper, I guess it made sense. I'd faked a blind act and then got myself rigged out in a cowboy outfit singing C&W songs. UA figured I'd gone, and thought another label could handle that. They could also earn a chunk of change before word got out that I'd turned into a fruitcake. They said, 'We don't even know you no more, Bobby. You're singing country and western. Motherfucker, you've gone.'

Columbia picked up my contract in 1976, and they wanted hits. They'd seen UA get some, so that's what they wanted. However, my view was I wasn't a guy that you could put in a bracket. Record companies wanted me to stick to the formula, the hit factory. They were only worried about the bottom line and hits. They didn't want any problems, someone doing something different. Did I want to open up a church and become a minister? Maybe, if God called me. The record labels couldn't handle that.

The execs would narrow their eyes and tell me, 'Bobby,

I hope God don't call because we really want you to cut some commercial stuff.'

The execs would get themselves in a spin about lyrics. They didn't like me using 'ass'. They thought I should substitute that with 'tush', told me 'tush' sounded better, more polite. I said, 'Fuck it, tush don't sound right. Whereas ass is beautiful with a melody and that's what I know my audience understands. They say ass. They don't say tush.'

I took myself off to Muscle Shoals again to work up *At Home In Muscle Shoals*. Columbia gave me the whip hand to produce two other albums: *Home Is Where The Heart Is* in 1976 and *Pieces* the following year.

But Columbia did not have the snap. I had the snap. When a company grows with you, like Minit, Liberty and UA had, they knew me. Columbia didn't know me, they'd just heard the records. They might have wanted to get to know me, but most times staff would change. Then there were reshuffles of the roster and political machinations.

I'm not even sure I got their trust. The company just wanted another 'Woman's Gotta Have It'. I started giving them songs like that, but I wasn't happy. Telling me to go out there and sing a song just like the last one, that's not where I was at. Not surprisingly, nothing really exceptional came of my time there.

Then I went to MCA/Arista. Came out with the *Roads Of Life* album in 1978, my final album of the 1970s. Not a big commercial success, but I may have been burned out.

CHAPTER 14
HANG ON IN THERE

I was married to Barbara about six years, right up to
1970. After that, I had a bunch of girlfriends, then, in
1976, I met the woman I'm still married to, although not
with: Regina Banks. She lives in New York and we have
a beautiful daughter, Ginaree.

One day I woke up, I had a great house and life was
good. I was still living a fast life. I was working, I was
partying, I had my friends, my lady friends, but my maid
Pecola, who was like a mother to me, thought I was
missing something.

On top of cleaning house, she also dispensed advice.
She said, 'Mr Womack, you know I haven't told you
anything wrong, but these people you know come up
here, drink all your liquor and eat all your food. This
place looks like a pigsty. And your car, the Rolls-Royce
Corniche, I'm surprised you still know you got it, the
dust is so thick on it.'

She had a point and she probably hadn't yet spied Sly

sleeping in the corner of the living room − on his head.

'Mr Womack,' she continued, 'you're a nice-looking man, if you just try. You need to get yourself a wife. You'd be surprised how your life will change if you got someone around you who really loves you.'

She had a plan too. 'I want you to get up, have a shave, comb your hair, get yourself a nice hot bath, scrape the dust off that Rolls and put the top down and go out and find yourself a nice woman.'

I was probably coming out from a bender so what Pecola said hit me. A wife? Yeah, that's exactly what I needed right then. That would sort me out.

So I went shopping. Washed the car − my little white two-seater Merc, not the Rolls − and off I went for a spin. I drove down Sunset Boulevard, just cruising, sat in that little sports car with my big old medallion on and a cowboy hat. I looked good, I thought. I also thought, 'Fuck this shit, I don't need a motherfucking wife, I need a drink.'

But, before I hit a bar, I spotted Regina. She was walking down the street with a white girlfriend. She was pretty, very pretty. So I slowed down and crawled along the kerb. I followed them. I smiled. I waved. I warmed up my charm offensive. 'Good evening, ladies,' I opened with. 'How you doing?'

I followed them all the way to where they were going, which was a gas station because Regina's girlfriend, Cathy, worked at the carwash there and was picking up a cheque.

I laid the charm on both girls, but especially spreading it thick with Regina. 'Why don't you all come round and we can have a drink and hang out,' I suggested.

Before I could open the car door, Regina's friend had leaped over it and jumped on my lap. Regina just stood there. I tried to figure a manoeuvre to get Regina in the car and on the seat next to me.

'Excuse me,' I said to the girl on my lap. 'Do you mind fetching me a carton of cigarettes?' When she got out, I told Regina to hop in and scoot over.

The three of us went on a little drive. They were best friends, I found out. We called around to a friend of mine's to pick up a little something, went back to my place and then I took them home. Like a gentleman.

The next time I saw Pecola, I was excited. I told her Regina might be the one. Naturally, she was surprised her project to find me a wife hadn't lasted longer than a day. She told me straight, 'Yeah, OK. But take it easy, you can't just go to the grocery store and get yourself a wife you only met a few hours ago.'

Something like the next day, I was out driving again, on Hollywood Boulevard, in the Rolls the time. I spotted a girl dressed in what looked like a nurse's uniform – white, white stocking, white shoes. I thought, 'Damn, that's exactly what I need, a nurse.' It was Regina again.

What a coincidence.

So I pulled over and called out, 'Hey, babe, how you doin'? Remember me?'

She didn't look as pleased as me. 'Oh, it's you again.'

I said, 'Yeah, I knew it was you. Where you heading?'

She was going to work. She wasn't a nurse, she was a waitress at the Holiday Inn.

'Look, you seem like a nice person, but I'm already seeing someone,' she told me.

That didn't discourage me. 'You could still see me too. I'm a nice guy.'

I pestered Regina all the way to the Holiday Inn, parked up and followed her in. She saw me again when she came out to serve customers. I was making a fuss wanting to be seated in her section. She had no option but to serve me.

'Oh God, it's you again,' she hissed. 'Why don't you get lost?'

'I'm already lost, I'm trying to get found.' I thought that sounded right. I kept at her, trying to make conversation and she was stuck because she couldn't be seen to ignore a paying customer. 'Oh, and you know what? I'll have a portion of French fries, crispy on the outside... what time do you get off?'

'What difference does it make? Nothing is going to happen here.'

I waited all day for her, on a mission now, until her shift finished. Slept a piece in the Rolls outside, lay down in the back seat with my feet up. When I woke it was with a start 'cos I thought I might have missed Regina. But then I spotted her, the working day over, walking out of the restaurant, past my car. She probably thought I'd given it up.

I'm pretty sneaky when I want to be so I let her get down the street and followed her all the way home, which was on Franklin, the street Janis OD'd on. I watched as Regina turned into an apartment block and disappeared up a flight of stairs. I started knocking on doors, trying to find her apartment. People would answer the door and find me standing there.

'Man, I don't believe this. Aren't you Bobby Womack?'

'Yeah, you can help me. Do you know a girl around here with brown skin, she dresses in white like a nurse?'

'You talking about Regina, she's up on the third floor, number 301.'

'Thanks, man.'

'Sure thing, Bobby.'

Up at 301 I could hear voices inside the apartment talking. 'He had on his big old medallion again, black hat this time and, oh, he had another car, Rolls-Royce, I think...'

I listened some more.

'That's right, I told him I was with someone; he said he wanted a nurse in his life. I think I got rid of him...'

I knocked on the door. This guy came to the door, a bottle of beer in his hand. The boyfriend, I guessed. I got the same reaction from him as I had at the apartments downstairs. 'Say, aren't you Bobby Womack?'

'Yeah, and I'm here to see Regina.'

'You know Regina?'

'Have done for years. We've been loving each other for a long time. I just thought she should maybe tell you this is happening between us because I can't do people like that.'

He tripped out on that. 'What the fuck are you talking about?' He shouted back into the living room. 'Hey, Regina, get out here, your boyfriend Bobby Womack is here.'

Now it was Regina's turn to be surprised. 'Oh my God, how did you find me?'

I asked her, 'Is this your boyfriend?'

She nodded. 'Yes.'

'Gina, baby, I can't hold it back, you better tell this man that we've known each other for months.'

I got myself inside the apartment. On top of Regina, there was Regina's sister and another girl. They were cracking up, but Regina didn't see the funny side, not right away. 'What are you talking about?'

'Regina, c'mon, don't play games.'

She exploded, told me to tell her fella that she didn't know me. There was a long silence as they waited for me to say something. I let them wait. Then I dropped on them.

'Baby, if that's your answer, then it is over.'

The boyfriend had had enough. He was mad. 'OK, I'm leaving,' he said. 'Give me my TV and get me a cab, it's over between us. I'm going back to Baltimore.' He packed his clothes. 'I can't believe you made up that story about him following you. How did he get here?'

Regina made a futile attempt to persuade him to stay. 'I don't know how he got here,' she said. 'He's lying, he's crazy, he don't even know me.'

But the boyfriend was out of there. When he was gone, she turned on me, let me have both barrels. 'I can't believe you've come into my house and ruined things like that.' She was real broke up. 'I can barely pay my rent...'

I had it all worked out. 'Yeah, sure, baby, but you can give this all up,' I told her, indicating the apartment. 'You know, I got a beautiful house up in the hills, it's all yours. Let's just drive up there.'

'I don't want to.'

'Well, I tell you what. I'm not leaving you. You are going to be my wife.'

Pecola couldn't have anticipated her plan was already in swing. And Regina couldn't believe my front. She ranted, 'My boyfriend has just left. What do you think I'm going to do?'

'Anyone who leaves that quick needs to leave,' I reasoned. 'He didn't even stand up and fight for you.'

'But you're a liar.'

'Yeah, maybe, but I would lie for someone like you.'

So it went back and forth like that for a while. Finally, Regina decided to call her mom. Got her on the phone and told her the story of the night. The mom asked if I was still around. Her daughter told her, 'Yeah, he's practically breathing down the phone.' The mother wanted to talk. Regina handed me the phone. 'She wants to speak to you.'

The mom got straight into it. Over the line, I was sprung a whole chunk of questions; stuff like: 'What do you want with my daughter?' I told her I wanted to marry her. 'How old are you?' I was 33 at the time.

'Well, do you know how old my daughter is? She just turned 18.' That was a legal age, I figured. 'Huh?'

'Look, I just want to marry her. I don't want to kidnap her.'

Then the mom started to soften up a bit. 'I just love your music.'

'OK.'

'What star sign are you?'

I knew I had her hooked then. 'I'm Pisces, lady.'

Would you believe it? She said, 'I'm Pisces too. You sound like you're kind of a crazy person, but I can tell you got a good heart. Put my daughter back on the line please.'

'OK, goodbye.'

So then the mom told Regina what Pisces is all about – spontaneity. Doing things on a whim, on the hoof, though not necessarily like finding a wife in a day. Mother and daughter argued a while and I made myself comfortable with one of the boyfriend's beers, earwigging the conversation and watching Regina's sister and girlfriend roll their eyes every time they didn't like where it was heading.

'It's too much too soon,' Regina told her mom. 'It's too sudden for me.'

God bless her mom. She must have told her that hooking up with me beat working at the Holiday Inn for tips.

'But I don't want to marry this guy for his money.'

Of course, the other girls were loving the whole

performance. They kept on at me to sing a song. 'Not right now, I'm trying to win this woman.'

After a while, Regina put her mom back on the phone. That went like this:

Mom: 'OK, Bobby, you really like my daughter, go buy her a wedding ring.'

Me: 'I can't just get one like that, she deserves a special stone.'

Mom: 'Uh-uh, well you get that wedding ring and then I'll see if you mean business.'

Me: 'I'm going away on tour for a couple of weeks, but I'll go to my jeweller and tell him I want a perfect pure diamond stone, blue, no yellow.'

Mom: 'OK, tell him to fix me one, too.'

I put the phone down and turned to my future wife, who said, 'See you when you get done with touring.'

'Get ready to get married,' I told Regina.

When I got back from the tour, I went to the jeweller and collected the stone. It came to something like $32,000: I had to sell a car to ante up the cash.

Regina and her mom had had plenty more chats by then and the gist was that if I got the ring then Regina would know I was serious. Her mom probably told her that if she didn't like me at least she could always get a divorce.

Regina asked me why we had to get married. I believed I could get her to love me later.

'OK,' she said. 'I'll get married to you but I'll never tell you I love you.' That's what I liked about her, she was honest. Said straight out it was crazy because she hardly knew me.

'That's all right. You'll get used to loving me in time. Get your things,' I instructed.

Regina moved into my house. Got the place decorated; brought in an interior designer who did a whole job getting rid of all my bachelor stuff – 'don't like this, don't like that' – and turned it into a couple's pad. She also told me to put a stop to all the women calling up still expecting the single Bobby Womack.

Then we had a sign made up: 'Please do not come by if you have not called and made an appointment. Thank you, Mr & Mrs Womack.'

Of course, we weren't married yet, but I soon fixed that. I called Rev James Cleveland who had a little Baptist church and had cut a few gospel numbers himself. I told Cleveland I was getting hitched. Told him I wanted to do it asap. 'I'm serious, I need your church Saturday. I'm getting married.'

'I don't know. We got prayer meeting and stuff.'

'James, we got to do it now or I might change my mind.'

We went through my address book and invited everyone. And everyone thought I had finally gone mad marrying a girl I hardly knew. On the way to the church, we told the limo driver to pull over and drop us off somewhere in the hills so we could take in the view before the ceremony. Two hours later, we woke up, late for our own wedding.

Over the next 18 years, we had some fun times. I was sat on my bed watching TV one night. The news came on and there was an item that interested me. It was sort of about me. It said the singer Bobby Womack had been arrested – with a stolen Rolls-Royce and a trunk full of cocaine.

They had film of the guy. He had his hands handcuffed behind him, funky threads and a pair of shades just like me, but he'd got one important detail down wrong. He was thin on top. Actually, he was totally bald.

I called my wife in. 'Hey, baby, come here. I've been arrested.'

Then the phone started ringing.

'I heard they got Bobby.'

'Oh, is it true?'

'They caught him?'

'He would never carry all that dope.'

My wife said, 'That's right, he's right here next to me in bed.'

So we called the TV station and I told them the guy that had been arrested was an impostor, a doppelganger. 'I am the real Bobby Womack,' I insisted.

Apparently, the guy had a fake driving licence with my picture and name in it. I went down to see him at the cop shop and asked him, 'Who are you, man?'

'I'm Bobby Womack.'

'No, man, wait a minute, *I'm* Bobby Womack.'

His line was: 'I'm not saying I am the *singer* Bobby Womack.'

By the time 1978 came around, we had a baby son on our hands. Sly Stone named him for us. Me and Sly were waiting outside the house one night for a delivery. I asked him what name I should give my son. He totally surprised me. He suggested The Truth. 'You should call him The Truth.'

'The Truth?'

'Yeah, Bobby. We tell so many lies so every time someone calls your son The Truth we got to do our part to live up to it and try and change.'

'Man, I ain't putting that name on him.'

'OK,' he said. 'Drop the "the" part and just call him Truth. Every time you do something or say you are then you have to – to stand up for your son, it means something.'

I said, 'Man, that's pretty cool.'

So we called our son Truth Bobby and I thought that was typical of Sly – heavy and totally unexpected, but right.

I suggested Truth to Regina, told her, 'Yeah, I'm going to change my life. I'm going to be truthful and everything. He's going to be living it.' She thought that was beautiful.

After Harry's death and the blind farrago, I was also back writing songs, and they were going well. If I worked late and things were running well, I'd wake up the wife, let her hear some of the work in progress. I said, 'Babe, I hate to wake you, but you got to hear this.' She used to like it. She would come down and listen while I sat there playing and trying to put something together.

One night, I got back to the house at about two or three in the morning. I went into the little studio I had and went through the same routine. Got my guitar and played a little, hoping something would come out. And it did. I thought up some chords, then crept into the bedroom where Regina and my little boy were sleeping. I whispered to her, asked her to get up. 'C'mon, I want to talk to you.' I told her to come into the studio I had out back of the house.

'Oh, Bobby,' she complained, 'it's four in the morning, I'm asleep.'

I was excited, and I pressed her. I kept on.

She told me she couldn't leave the infant. She said, 'Bobby, the baby is crawling in his sleep.'

I insisted. 'Look, he's asleep, he can barely move.' I didn't let up.

We went out back and I poured a couple of glasses of champagne. We can't have been in there more than two minutes, maybe less. Regina sat down, but she was anxious to keep an eye on the baby, so I said I'd fetch him. I ran back to the bedroom.

When I got there what I saw made me freeze. The baby – he was only four months old – had crawled all the way up to the top of the bed, but there was no headboard. Truth Bobby had fallen, and he was wedged down between the bed and the wall. His little feet were blue and they were cold. I went into shock. I was so scared. I was terrified.

I said, 'Oh, God.' I snatched him up and shook him, but

it was too late. They had him on a respirator at the hospital, but he had suffocated.

I always said it was a crib death. It put a dark cloud over the rest of my life. Regina's too. It was a cloud that never lifted. I blamed myself. I was older than my wife, much older. If only I hadn't gone in to wake her up.

Even though we tried to make it up or put it behind us over the years, there was always the nagging thought that if I had never asked her to come out to the studio it wouldn't have happened. The hurt was always there and we became more distant after that.

We buried Truth Bobby in the crypt next to Sam Cooke. We also moved out of the house. Regina wouldn't stay in the same place her firstborn had died. The pain was too much, seeing the baby's room that she'd had freshly painted. The strain started to tell.

Regina came into my life and totally turned it upside down, but in a positive way. She was pushing and I knew she was trying to make positive changes, but sometimes when you've been spoiled for a lot of your life you are where you are because you want to be there. You expect everyone to just get in line. Regina wasn't ready to fall in line.

One thing she told me, she said I was prejudiced. She lectured me, 'You talk about how the white man has fucked you up, but you are just as prejudiced.'

That was true. I wanted to be macho, like my father had taught me. I hated gays. When I was a kid, my father told me, 'Gay men are weird. Any man bent over is wrong. God didn't make it like that, it is a mistake.' It was the way I was brought up, calling them sissies.

Even my old manager Ed Wright caught it from me. Ed and me had been real close. He was my manager for years. After The Valentinos broke up, he quit his radio show in Cleveland to come and work with me.

We got on well, but then Barbara told me he was gay. That came as a total shock. I didn't believe it, but I called him on it. He told me he was gay. I accused him of fucking me around. So he said, 'What? You don't like me any more?' I thought about that. He had been afraid to show me his real side because he thought I would disown him.

Regina had a friend called David who was gay. I hated David. I thought that come the night David would become a straight man, that his dick would get as hard as mine with a woman, and he would get it on with my wife. I thought he was making me look stupid.

Of course, my wife dismissed this, told me that David would be insulted if she tried anything on with him. Said they were just good friends. This went on and on. They would get drunk over at his place and David would call to tell me she was staying over because she couldn't drive home.

I said, 'Sure, sure,' but I didn't believe it. This wound me up and one time I told her I wanted her to come home. No matter what. I threatened to come right through David's door if she didn't. I had to go and fetch her. David said, 'Oh, I love your music.'

225

I said, 'Fuck that.' I was there for my wife.

We ended up arguing. I didn't want her around gay people, said it was hurting our marriage, although it was me doing that.

Any time there was a gay guy up at our house I would leave. It was really childish.

After we lost Truth Bobby, Regina and David became closer still. Then, about six months after the baby's death, she took some pills. She was frustrated with me.

I found her in bed, tried to lift her, but she was like a dead weight. When I finally got her up and out of the bed I was worried about getting her dressed because I didn't want doctors, the ambulance crew, anyone, seeing her like that. Man, I didn't know how fucked up I was.

I called a maid for help and tried to dress her, put her panties on, bra, everything. The maid said, 'You are wasting time here. Just put on a gown. C'mon.'

When the doctors finally got a look at her, they were worried it might be too late because she did not initially respond to treatment. Even if they did revive her, she could still have suffered some damage. She had tubes in her, her eyes were open, but she wasn't there.

I was desperate. I called David and told him my wife was in a coma. He flew right over in his car. David and I sat there. I didn't know if I would see my wife again. I said, 'This is what it takes to bring us together, a gay man and a straight man.'

He told me that Regina had tried to do what I wanted, but he and the other gay guys were her friends. Why should she be made to feel bad about bringing them home? He said that just because I did drugs – he didn't do them – didn't mean he disliked me.

I said, 'You know, David, I'm a fucking asshole. I was taught prejudice. No gay man has ever done me wrong or bothered me. I was taught by my father it was wrong.' We hugged, I told him I loved him. I told David I wanted to be his friend.

I was worried about Regina. When I consulted a doctor, his advice was simple. He told me to try for another baby. 'Get her pregnant, otherwise you are going to lose her.' I said I thought I had already lost her.

A few weeks later, Regina complained of feeling sick, nauseous. I said, 'Really? I can't understand that. Why don't you go and check it out?' Man, she screamed so loud when the doctor told her she was pregnant. When our other baby came, we kept the name Truth, just changed it around from Truth Bobby to Bobby Truth.

So Bobby Truth, maybe that's why he had some problems. He would ask me, 'Did you just have me to replace the other baby?' Sometimes I can understand why he ended up in jail.

When Bobby Truth first arrived, I used to take him on the road. I gave him a little fake guitar and he would dress like me, came on stage playing. Vincent, my son with Barbara, was also around then.

Vincent didn't want to go to school, he had everything he wanted, but he wore his mom out. He didn't finish school and I don't think he was able to deal

227

with all the money and fame. I know women took money from him and ran; women didn't want to be with him, but everyone had a plan for him – 'you should do this, you should do that'. They would constantly be on him, ragging on him. They said things like, 'You're Bobby Womack's son? But you don't sing, you don't do nothing.'

He said, 'I'm not a singer.' Vincent would get high and if he had one little drink or one little anything it was like he had tons of it. He became a totally different person. He was trying to find a way to die.

He found one. Vincent committed suicide when he was 21: he put a bullet in his head. I had everything and whatever he didn't have I didn't or couldn't give to him. I can't tell you when he died; I blanked it out.

After Vincent died, I noticed Bobby would sleep with Vincent's picture all the time. He had a lot of questions about why Vincent killed himself. He said to me, 'Dad, hey, if you hadn't been a music man and been able to live a normal life and been with Vincent, would he have done that to himself?' Damn, that was a tough question.

I was the kind of person who didn't want to get fucked up in the street or on stage. I didn't want to embarrass my fans, but when I went home? I did the damage behind closed doors. I got so far into the drug shit, I couldn't go back. I owed it to Bobby because I lost two boys being ignorant, but I was still in so much pain.

Pain, drugs and guns don't mix, though. I had the first two in spades and, after we got robbed at the house one time, we got ourselves a couple of guns, too, one for me, one for the wife.

When it got to the point of doing drugs constantly, more than I should have, it got like people thought I had big money. I was also worried about being busted, always thought I would be busted. It was a serious fear; however, it's one thing I've not done. I've never gone to jail or embarrassed anyone. That was important to me. I didn't want to be seen by my family walking through the house with my hands behind my back, handcuffed.

I always had a gun right where I could get my hands on it, wherever I was. Hotel or home, it didn't matter, the gun would be there. This went on for about ten years of my life: I called them the paranoia years, and I was severely paranoid. No one could make any noise in the house in case it woke up the neighbourhood. I was always keyed up. Couldn't even say, 'Pass the toot', for fear that someone would hear me. They had to pass the candy.

One day, I was propped up in bed. It was between night and morning, still dark. I was tired. I was paranoid. *Very* paranoid. I saw the handle on the door to the bedroom slowly turn. Burglar? House invasion? Shit, I didn't think. I couldn't think straight. All I saw was the door begin to open. I reached for my gun and emptied it into the door. Pow, pow, pow, pow.

The door, riddled with gunshots, pushed open wide and my little boy, Bobby Truth, not yet into long trousers, ran in as if nothing had happened. He came into the room, jumped up to his mom beside me and lay down for a cuddle. All the bullets had gone straight over his head.

Regina threatened to leave after that. I begged her not to, said I would straighten out. I put the gun away and left it away.

The first time Bobby Jr got in trouble we were living up in the Hollywood Hills. He and a little friend of his went through everybody's mailbox in the neighbourhood, took all the mail out and threw it away. A security guard who patrolled around there arrested him or put some handcuffs on him, just to try and scare him, tell him it was wrong.

Just like Vincent, Bobby was very hard-headed, didn't want to go to school, started getting into more serious things. He said he was in gangs, told me he was initiated – had to fight and get beat up to become a member. I told him, 'Bobby, you don't need to be no gang member. Those guys have a lot of problems. I can't see how you're going to fit in. You're trying to talk different; you're trying to sound tough and you the only one getting caught.'

So he wound up in jail a few times. The first time he was in a stolen car; he wasn't driving, but it wasn't his car. He was sentenced and did some time. He was only about 11 or 12 years old so it was youth custody, not really jail, but he was locked up. That was hard for me. I would go and visit all the time. Every weekend I had to drive almost 100 miles to make it up to see him.

Later, he was always coming around with beat-up old

cars that I would end up paying for. He said they were in perfect shape, but they never ran. So then he was off driving my car. Told me stuff like, 'Dad, just stay out of my business.'

Straight back I said, 'I'd love to stay out of your business, but you always cost me money, you break my heart, man. You go to jail and I don't feel right seeing you in jail.'

One time I had a Cadillac restored, one he wanted, I had it all worked on. Told the Caddy people, 'Make this car just like it was when it came off the line.' I told Bobby, 'All I want you to do is go to school, you don't have to worry about it, you know I give you money every week; all I want is for you to do something with your life.'

But he messed around with that car, had people rip him off. Told me someone had stolen his tyres. That car ended up broke down, too, on the freeway. People had ripped him off, ripped me off.

I don't know what it was. I never robbed, I never stole, I'm from the old school, my father taught me right. I would get out of the car to open the door for a woman, but my boy Bobby just seemed to be the total opposite. I couldn't understand why it was like that. I didn't see my brothers' sons behaving like that. We used to argue all the while about his music – he listened to nothing but rap. I would have been happy if he had wanted to join a rap group. I like rap music, but only if it is telling kids something constructive, being used as a political tool or telling them what they have to do to survive in this world.

I come down on men who give women babies and then slip off saying they're just popping out for a loaf of bread. That ain't a man. Also, kids will come across stuff like drugs, but don't encourage it on record. It's like me saying, 'Do drugs, they are great.' A kid's mind is like clay and you can mould it. So you got to be careful and respect that.

With my son, if there was talent in him I would have loved that to come out, but it won't come out because someone forces you. It won't come out because you want to prove a point. It comes out because that was something you really wanted to do.

The second time Bobby went away was after I gave him $500. It was one Christmas. I wanted him to take the money and buy his mom and sister gifts. I told him, 'Do that and the rest you can have for yourself, you know, whatever you want to do with it.' He went and bought a gun.

He took his new gun over to a shopping mall to buy the gifts. Evidently, he got distracted and wanted to use the payphone. The problem was there was already a guy using it. He ran up to the guy talking and put the gun to his head, told him to get off the phone. Bobby told him, 'Hey, I want to use the phone.'

I think he was trying to be a big shot. Something like that, did he do it just to find out what it felt like? If you pull a gun on someone, they have nothing to lose.

When I found out about that, I was disgusted. I said, 'It's Christmas. Take him. I don't want to see him.' So I knew what it meant when parents asked how their kids ended up dead or in gangs. My kid had the best of life, the best of living. All I wanted him to do – and all I preached to him – was go to college, get an education. I quit school, got educated the hard way, and it probably cost me millions of dollars because that's what it cost with all the attorneys, managers, all those kinds of people taking money from me.

The third jail time was because he robbed a Thrifty's Drug Store. He was the lookout man, the one standing outside watching for the cops. They got the money, drove about a block around the corner, pulled up and sat in the car counting it out – seeing how much they got. The police came right up on them.

Bobby jumped out and ran off with a gun, but he ran into a corner with nowhere to hide. He ducked behind a car and a cop talked him out, said he didn't want to end up killing him. After a while, Bobby threw his gun out. Man, he must have been scared. He got three years for that. His friend went down too, a quiet, easy-going guy, real nice, but they became different people after jail. Bobby was released on parole, but next thing he was in a stolen car, ran a light and crashed into another car. He killed the other driver.

They got him down for second-degree murder and sent him down for 28 years. That's a long stretch. My son said to me one time, 'I'm locked up and I got nothing to do but stare at these four walls and think about everything.' Everything that went wrong.

233

In the middle of all this, my dad died. One morning he called and said he needed to see me, wanted to talk. He was already in hospital, had been for a time. 'I'll wait on you,' he said.

When I put the phone down, I turned to Regina and told her he was gonna die. I dressed up like I was going to the office, put on a suit, tie, the whole bit. When I walked into the hospital, I saw Momma. She told me he was waiting on me. The doc told us Dad had the body of an 80-year-old man, but he was nowhere near that. He was just plain worn out.

I went into the ward and he was laid on his stomach. He told me to come around the bed so he could take a look at me. When I did, he grabbed my hand. He said, 'I want to see you before I go. I know what it took you to get over Harry's death. I want you to know I lived another year just for your mother, to prepare her. Your mother is like a little girl because I never let her grow. I want you to take my place and look out for your mom and do all the things she wants to do.'

A little while later, Dad was given a shot. That triggered something and he started coughing. A hideous, thick yellow film came over his eyes. Man, that freaked me out. A doctor came in and they drew the curtains. Then I heard a nurse. She said, 'He's gone, he's gone.' When I heard that, I ran out of the place as fast as I could.

I've had some bad luck with death, people who died around me, so I shut it off. All those people who died, it fucked my head up. After a while I thought, 'I can't take

234

this.' Some people, it don't matter what you do for them, will mess up. I stopped holding on to the guilt.

I always wanted a little girl, always wanted one. I told Regina, 'Babe, boys don't turn out too good.' We had a girl and we called her Ginaree.

CHAPTER 15

THE POET

In my time, I've been called a few names. Nobinee, Stack, by Pickett, and The Poet. That caught on after I cut an album in 1980 and called it *The Poet*.

Some people call it my comeback album after all the squabbling over *BW Goes C&W* and my departure from UA/Liberty. Columbia, MCA, they'd been OK, but by the end of the 1970s I was without a record deal.

I turned around and Wilton Felder, the bass and sax man of the Crusaders, asked me to be a guest vocalist on his solo album *Inherit The Wind*. The song was a hit and got the attention of a guy called Otis Smith, who was promoting the Crusaders.

Otis Smith I had heard of. He'd been around the business a long time as a record label executive, and was good at what he did. A good promotions man, too. Then Smith started his own venture, Beverly Glen. He named the label after that big long boulevard that snakes down from Sherman Oaks, through the Hollywood Hills, Bel Air and down south of Westwood.

Smith's pitch was pretty good. He said that the white man had been taking money from the black artist for too long. I wasn't signed with anyone, so I got myself a new label. Me and Smith talked about how it would work out. One suggestion was that I could have done a job scouting, helping to bring some acts to the outfit. I had resurfaced mentally and spiritually. I was happy.

Later, Johnny Taylor, who replaced Sam Cooke in the Soul Stirrers and recorded for his SAR and Derby labels, joined and had a record out on Beverly Glen. Anita Baker, the female lead singer of Chapter 8, who Smith worked with, also recorded her first album, *The Songstress*, for his label in 1983.

I went in the studio on my own and started recording. I put the whole band together. I had Patrick Moten on keyboards, who I met through Ike Turner. He helped produce the album with me (he'd also helped produce Anita's first album). Guitar was me and David T Walker; James Gadson on drums, and David Shields and Nathan East sharing bass. It was all guys that I knew could come right in and also bring something to the table. Curtis helped out on vocals, and Regina and Vincent were both in there somewhere with handclaps.

We cut the stuff in a few days. When you've got ideas and you know where you're going, it don't take that long. I even got my brother Cecil in to help, and we were fighting. I also did his song, 'Just My Imagination'.

Eight tracks; the album started with 'So Many Sides Of You' and finished on 'Where Do We Go From Here'.

Somewhere between them is 'If You Think You're Lonely Now', which is one of the stand-out tracks and one of the album's hits.

The Poet came out in 1981. It was hailed as a masterpiece. That was about as far as it did work out, because the next bit was a real blow. I didn't get paid. The album was selling tens of thousands, then hundreds of thousands, but nothing was coming my way, very little anyway. Smith looked at me as a worn-out junkie, somebody who had talent but didn't know who he was. He disrespected me.

I asked Smith for something like $50,000 against future royalties. He told me he'd get back to me the next day. I didn't get that 50 grand, nowhere near it. Then I saw Otis Smith less and less. The next time I saw him he was in court.

It took nearly three years for the case to go through the legal process. It was a really drawn-out battle and the bills kept stacking up. Attorneys would leave the case, new ones would join. I spent so much time in that damn courthouse I ended up writing a song there.

I had my day, week and month in court. Gave my evidence and sat and watched Smith deliver his. Watched and heard several versions of the truth come out. Then at the end of each very long day I would go back to the Beverly Hills Hotel, have a drink – a cocktail – order dinner and then go through the strategy plan for the following day's session. I'd order wine, go over it. Do some more preparation during mains, finish that and then work on it again through dessert. I used to do all that every single evening after court finished. And I had a dinner companion. That was Allen Klein.

Allen Klein is a shrewd, sharp businessman. Allen also has a lot of heart. That's something I know. He might not be a singer or a writer, but he can take a song across the world just as easily.

When I first knew Allen Klein, in the early 1960s, he was Sam Cooke's accountant. Allen was young then – and fat. He wore one blue suit and a stripy tie. The suit used to shine so much you could use it as a mirror.

He was the kind of guy who didn't care how much you pushed him away. He would keep coming back time and again, like a bee on honey. JW Alexander was around then, but JW was not as smart as Allen. Smart and aggressive, a real go-getter, Allen was also white, which helped in dealing with the predominantly white-run record labels.

Sam admired Allen's chutzpah. I think Sam thought, if he kept his end up, then Allen would take care of the rest of it. What impressed me about Allen was that Sam always worried about what he had to say: what he thought about the show, what he thought about this, what he thought about that, what he had to say about his life – period.

Allen would never come in the dressing room after the show and say it was fantastic. He'd only be there to tell Sam what the problem, or problems, were. Tell him the show sucked, that the third song shouldn't have been there or that the outfit wasn't making it. He was the only guy who did that.

Sam would tell him to get the fuck out of there. He'd chase him out. Sam told him, 'You don't know the fucking problem. You don't sing, you don't do this, get out of here, man. I don't want to hear no criticism from you.' Even then, Allen would keep at it with the criticism. It's easy to get yes men around, but Allen wasn't one of them.

Allen's remarks would bug Sam. He'd go back home and they'd nag at him. Sam would ask me what I thought about what Allen had said. That got me thinking. I thought, 'If Sam spends this much time worrying about what Allen is up to, Klein must mean something to him.'

He did. They got tight when Allen bet Sam he could find some money for him. Cash that the labels or publishers owed Sam, but hadn't passed on. Just let it lie in a drawer.

Sam didn't believe Allen at first, told him to get out of there. We were all naive back then, expected to be paid by the business, but Allen persisted. He kept whispering in his ear about that missing money, told Sam about audits. He said, 'There is gold in them hills.' And there was: he turned up with something like $100,000.

Sam was shocked at how much cash had been swilling around, cash that was his by rights, and he was very interested in Allen after that. And the moves Allen made. He gave him a piece of the real action then and that put Allen on the management track.

Barbara had sold some of Sam's publishing to Allen. I did the same a few years later so Klein and his company, ABKCO Music, became my publisher. They didn't get all my songs, but enough, including a lot of the songs from *The Poet*.

That was something else I regretted. At the time – I sold it in the 80s – Allen advised me against it. I wanted to lay my hands on some big money and fast, but Allen told me not to sell. He said the publishing, my writing, had no price. It was priceless. He also told me it would take care of me for life.

I didn't listen, so Allen told me that whichever publishing company won out with the highest bid, he would triple it. Don't know why I didn't ask for a loan, but I have too much pride. I wouldn't want to ask somebody for something without giving them some sort of collateral. That collateral was my songs, my songwriting, my life.

One time I told Allen, 'Money don't mean nothing to me.' I was angry about something. That was my statement. Allen told me that scared him. He was afraid of that kind of talk. And I never forgot that.

Allen Klein was at the Womack versus Smith court sessions every day. Then he had dinner with me after and discussed the case, every night.

Allen would give me advice like, 'Bobby, you are in court now, don't give them nothing to elaborate on. Just answer yes or no.'

Allen would get tired, he'd have rings under his eyes, but he told me, 'I never quit, I never quit at anything.'

I didn't care for Smith. Often he would be in court and

he would whisper these snide asides. Man, that wound me up tight, but I got a crack at him. Literally. I punched him out. One day outside the courtroom, I landed one on his jaw and knocked him down. I drew my fist back so far to punch Smith that I hit his attorney, too. Smashed him with my elbow, knocked him over, then swung for Smith and put him down too. His lawyer threatened to sue me for assault.

While this was going on, Smith was still selling the album and making deals because he had the master tapes. What I did then wasn't strictly legal, but I was desperate. I stole back my masters.

I knew Smith had them locked up in a warehouse in LA. I called it up, lied and told them I was Otis Smith. I said, 'Hey, this is Otis. I'm sending Bobby Womack by to pick up the masters, he wants to go in and redo some things on them.'

The warehouse guy said, 'No problem, Mr Smith.'

I got the tapes and then called up Smith. 'You ain't paid me no money,' I said.

He gave me some bull about how he had reignited my career when I was down and out and that I was ungrateful.

I listened to that. Then I told him about the tapes. I said, 'What would you say if I told you that you don't have to give me the kiss of life now because I just stole those tapes back?'

That got his attention. He couldn't believe it and begged for them back.

I said, 'Goodbye, Otis,' put the phone down and smiled for the first time in months.

In court, we won the music rights back, but the judge ordered me to hand over the masters, said those tapes were Smith's by law. It didn't make sense, but I had my fun.

The Poet was the most successful album I ever had, but typically a lot around it turned out bad. *The Poet* brought me back, but I could have done without Otis Smith.

Our contractual dispute put me a little behind track, but I finally broke free of Smith and Beverly Glen and got around to putting out *The Poet II* in 1984, this time through Motown. I brought Patti LaBelle on for that.

I was on the road, performing in Philadelphia, and Patti came to sing with me. We demolished the house. After that, I said we should collaborate and asked her to do a guest shot on my album.

We ended up duetting on three tracks, including 'Love Has Finally Come At Last'. I knew if we put that song out it would be a smash record; it was.

That wasn't the last I heard of Smith. Beverly Glen cashed in on the success of *The Poet* a year later when it released an album culled from my sessions, *Someday We'll All Be Free*.

I'm a firm believer that when people do you wrong they catch it somewhere down the line. I don't know what happened to Smith, but I heard he wasn't in the music business any more.

CHAPTER 16

HARLEM SHUFFLE

After Sam died, Ronnie Wood became my closest friend. I would – and could – talk to Woody if there was a problem.

Wherever he was – at home, on tour – he never changed. He was just a guy. Silly sometimes, never any pressure, not like a lot of musicians I hung with. I could never get close to them because they would never let you in; they put this aura around themselves.

We first met when The Faces called me to support them on their last tour. I first heard of Rod Stewart in 1966. He had just recorded a version of Sam Cooke's 'Shake'. It wasn't Sam, but it wasn't bad neither.

Four years later – and like the Stones before him – Rod taped my song 'It's All Over Now'. That helped give my career a kick. Then, another four years after that, in 1974, The Faces sounded me out about being their support act.

Woody got me on the phone, handed it to Rod and he

grilled me. Wanted to know what sort of cigarettes Sam Cooke smoked. Told him L&Ms. What did he drink? Told him martini cocktails. Or Beefeater gin.

I got the tour. What I didn't know then was it would be the last hurrah by The Faces. And the outing would also enter the annals of legendary alcohol and substance abuse.

At the start, I could never tell the difference between Woody and Rod. They both just looked alike to me, both had their hair in a little shag. I guess Ronnie was a little more outgoing of the pair. They were a good bunch. They wanted to know how I got my voice raspy. I told them it was singing with bad microphones first, then hipped them to the Jack Daniel's. The trick: take a swig just before going on stage, then gargle.

Next time I saw them, they're passing around a bottle of Jack, taking a slug and going 'ga-ga-ga'. I asked them what they were doing.

'You're the one that told us.'

'What?'

'To gargle.'

I laughed. 'Man, I was just bullshitting you. You can't do that with bourbon, that'll tear your fucking throat out.'

'So, what do you do with it?'

'I dunno about you, man,' I said, 'but Jack Daniel's, I drink that shit.'

So that was it with me and The Faces, they would be up playing jokes on everyone. Dumb stuff like stomping up the toilets and flooding the bathroom, putting gum in the keyholes. They partied a lot. If they didn't get thrown out of a hotel it wasn't fun.

So I did that last tour with The Faces. I liked them. Rod had wanted me on it so I could do a couple of Sam Cooke songs with him, like 'Bring It On Home To Me' and 'I'm Having A Party'.

Woody told Rod that he now had a good reason to do the Cooke songs because I had a direct link to the man. I thought it would be good if I made that tour, but the way it went was Rod called me out, I did the two songs and that was it. I was bored waiting back there when I was all fired up, so I also played guitar in the band.

I picked up a vibe that there was arguing between the band from the start. The band was accompanied by an 18-piece string section: someone told me this was Rod's idea, that he wanted to do it his way or no way. The band wasn't so keen and it meant tempers were frayed.

It didn't help that Rod remained isolated throughout much of the tour. He and his then girlfriend, Britt Ekland, travelled separately. When they checked into hotels, they used the alias Mr and Mrs Cockforth.

On top of the personal beefs within the band, there was a whole army of journalists who had attached themselves to that circus. Media conferences became the norm, sometimes with Britt holding court while Rod silently seethed. One particularly pushy pressman had his note pad torn up and thrown in his face by an enraged Rod.

The band's antics meant that the tour manager had a headache getting them into hotels as they'd been banned by the Holiday Inn chain. Some nights he resorted to booking rooms as Fleetwood Mac.

Despite that, there was still mayhem. In one hotel, the management were caught between accommodating Rod and Britt and Helen Reddy and her husband. Reddy was due to check into the penthouse suite. The problem was it hadn't been cleaned and it was still occupied by The Faces singer and his girlfriend. The desk clerk tried to hurry Rod on his way. Big mistake.

Rod, the rest of the band and the roadies took the matter into their own hands. On Rod's command, everyone ripped into the suite for the next 20 minutes destroying the bed, smashing the TV and anything else that wasn't nailed down.

Throughout the tour, there were rumours that Rod would be quitting. Then, Ronnie confided in me that it was going to be the last Faces tour. He said, 'Rod is leaving, he ain't taking me with him.' I asked what was going to happen with the rest of the guys and he said, 'I don't know, man, but this is it.'

Next thing I heard Ronnie Wood was going to join the Rolling Stones. That was a good gig. We were close by then so he asked me to go to Paris with him to meet Mick Jagger, negotiate his deal joining the group. He was going to replace Mick Taylor, who had replaced Brian Jones. Mick was with Bianca Jagger at the time. We visited them in a hotel.

Ronnie asked me, 'What do you think I should ask them for?'

248

I said, 'Man, I don't know. I never thought about the money they make. Ask them for a million dollars.'

'You think that much?'

I didn't really know. 'Just a million to get started with it,' I instructed, but I really didn't know what I was talking about because I didn't know how everything worked. 'Just listen to what Mick is talking about,' I advised, 'and sit there with him and let him tell you what he is going to do, and then you can say you will get back to him.'

It was years and years before Woody became a full Stone. And he had it rough. Anything they wanted to dump, they dumped it on Woody. I guess after Jones they wanted to be sure – make it so no one would take a piece of the pie and then find they couldn't get rid of him.

Ronnie is just a sweetheart of a guy, and if he was in your corner he was in your corner all the way. He always tried to bring people together, to stop the bickering and fighting.

Keith took Woody under his arm. Keith had been with a lot of guitar players, but to play together you almost have to live together. Keith could get that out of Woody, and Woody was willing to give him that. They built a strong, powerful relationship and that kept Woody in the group.

Keith Richards was a true warrior and a very soulful guy. He was frank: if Keith didn't like someone, they would know it right away. He reminded me of somebody in my neighbourhood, like a little ghetto kid who is just mad 'cos he's in the ghetto and he is going to kill anybody who looked better than him. Keith had that attitude, but if he liked you he was real cool.

One time Keith was mad at me. Didn't speak to me for a while. I think he thought that anything that fucked with Woody or got him in trouble was down to me, 'cos we were close. Keith's attitude was: 'Why is Womack always there? He's part of the problem.'

The Stones had recorded 'It's All Over Now', but I wasn't around for that and didn't run into the band properly until a decade later when I hooked up to do a couple of tours with them in the mid-1970s. Their cover had been my greatest crossover record. The Stones had made my name in 1964; I was somebody. I also thought they believed I was some kind of unsung hero to them. They had tried to be everyone else in those early years, one day James Brown, the next Jackie Wilson, anyone who came into the city they would try out.

So maybe they had me on the tours because they knew I had heart and never lost it. I wasn't the only artist working those 1970s tours. Prince was out there one time, this was way before *Purple Rain*. He was just getting known and working up the crowd for the Stones. The guy was having an orgasm with his guitar.

Word got back that the audience might not have been appreciating Prince's act as much as he thought. Two roadies were instructed to throw him off the stage, and that's what they did: walked on in the middle of his performance, grabbed him and literally threw him under a piano. Prince went sailing off and out into the wings.

At least I knew the punishment the Stones had in store for not coming up to scratch, but sometimes I thought the band just brought me out for amusement – to hear my jokes. There would be times when I was out with them, but not performing. Woody called up and said, 'You come out, how long can you stay with us?'

I told him, 'Woody, I ain't got no job, I ain't in that kind of good shape. I'm a legend – not a rich legend, a broke legend.' He promised me a suite. 'You got a room, we'll get some money, we'll rub some nickels together.'

I said, 'Nickels don't sound like a whole lot of money.'

They took care of me, took care of anything I wanted. Woody would tell me, 'You know you'll have money; it's good for Keith, it's good for Charlie, it's good for everybody.' So I would be with them on tour, but not working. And I thought, 'This is weird. They just want me for a spiritual vibe. I ain't an artist here, more like a priest.'

That was kind of tough because I'm a singer; I'm in the same business as the Rolling Stones, but what was I doing being a priest? They were all on stage and I wanted to be out there with them. We'd play music after the shows. Just sang songs. Keith was always up on guitar players all the way back to Robert Johnson. He knew everybody from jazz to classical players. You name it, he was into it. He also got some nice pockets. Keith would play me songs and I'd ask him to give me the song. Keith didn't go for that. 'This is for the band, you fuck. Don't you dare try and catch me at a weak moment and take one of our songs.'

251

So, I said, 'Man, write me one, then.'

If I was on the bill, sometimes I would go on stage to sing 'It's All Over Now'. And I could feel the audience – all 100,000 people or whatever – stop and look. I knew they wondered who the motherfucker was singing a Rolling Stones song, and it was my song. I thought, 'Hey, man, I could kill the house if only I was on my side of town.'

One time I was hanging with the Stones and I had my own album out. I was all proud, but it wasn't getting airplay. The band asked, 'Do you think you are going to cross over on this one. Bobby?'

'Yeah,' I said, 'it had better cross over or I'll end up falling over.'

A phone call came in to the Stones camp and for some reason I picked it up. It was the boss of MTV and he was trying to get the Rolling Stones for an interview. He said, 'Who's this?' I told him. 'Oh, Bobby, what a brilliant album you got.'

'Yeah, it's so brilliant, why aren't you playing it?'

The guy went into a spiel and told me to get a copy over. I told him no. 'I ain't getting it over there, I sent 10,000 copies already.'

So he reeled me in with a deal: if I hooked MTV up with one of the Stones for an interview, then I'd get some heavy rotation on his station.

I told Keith and Woody. They both agreed to do the interview, but would only talk up my album when they got there. They made the company pick us up in separate limos, police on all sides, and also pick up the tab. I thought, 'Man, with all these limos and stuff, they'll never play my record now. This was more than it cost to make the album.'

In the studio, the interview was wild. They said things like, 'The man here [me] has cut an album you say doesn't fit your format – what fits your fucking format?'

MTV got the record on and everything, but I walked away from that thinking it was not about my music, it was about the colour of my skin. Still was.

I played on the Stones' album *Dirty Work*. Recorded it in Paris and New York in 1985, did 'Harlem Shuffle'.

The group thought I might be a good inspiration, thought it would be cool. I worked mostly with Keith and Ronnie; they would lay down the tracks and I would do the backgrounds. Those guys would call me the Womack Sisters because I could sing all the high parts like a couple of chicks.

It was a good album. Keith and Woody were tight. They worked together. Where Keith went, Woody went. But the band weren't working as a unit. There were a lot of stumbling blocks. No real communication, for a start. Charlie didn't seem to be feeling well most of the time and I never really saw Bill Wyman. He did his parts mostly when no one else was around. Mainly it seemed like it was all business. The vibe in the studio wasn't right. The two main players in the group are Mick and Keith, but they weren't talking. They never really got together.

If Mick spoke with me the rest of the group were curious to know what he said. Not that Mick said a whole lot to me anyway, although one time he decided he wanted to take a stroll down Broadway. Mick said, 'C'mon, Bobby, forget getting a cab, let's walk.' As if no one would recognise Mick Jagger.

It was fine for a minute. No one had spotted him. Then I heard a rumble, turned around and saw a herd of people. Thousands of them and all running towards us. And gaining – fast.

Mick shouted, 'Let's go,' and we ran. We sprinted right across the street to a Japanese joint. Jagger knocked like crazy on that restaurant door and, fortunately, the owner recognised him. He opened the door, we fell inside, the door was locked and the crowd stayed shut out.

Mick suggested we order up some sushi, give it time for the fans to drift off. Now, sushi ain't my thing. I said I didn't want to eat raw fish, I'd go for the tempura, but the menu had the sushi coming in at around five dollars, and the tempura was more expensive.

Mick insisted, 'Let's have the sushi.'

'Nah, tempura for me.'

'Sushi.'

It went back and forth like that. Finally, Mick said, 'OK, I'll buy you the tempura and you pay for the limo back to the hotel.'

Man, I was shocked, but I made the deal. It was a bum deal, though. I'd rather have paid for two dinners.

That wasn't the only strange Mick Jagger thing. We recorded 'Harlem Shuffle' together. He said, 'Womack, will you teach me how to sing soul?'

I told him, 'I'm still trying to learn how to sing it. I couldn't teach you in a couple of hours.'

He always teased me about my style, where I talked a little before singing. I would always do a little speech, tell people what the song was about. Jagger would laugh and said, 'Bobby ain't going to sing no song unless he gives you a sermon first, tell us what the song is going to be about.'

Sure, brother. 'That's it, like a preacher man.'

We did the track. I was really singing in there with him. 'Yeah, yeah, yeah, do the Harlem Shuffle, do the monkey shine.' I thought, 'Man, this will be a good shot for me.'

Jagger told me, 'You sing the top part and I'll sing the bottom and a little bit in the middle.'

When I heard the track played back after, all of that had gone. I was basically in fade. You could hear my voice, no one could take that off, but it had been faded way, way down. Maybe that's what he meant when he asked me to teach him how to sing soul: 'I'll study what Womack does on the vocal and then put mine on it.'

There would be a few other beefs too. Trivial shit, but hurtful. When I got through singing or doing my thing at the studio – and that was well into the night or morning sometimes – I'd be beat. I'd leave, go to take the limo parked outside for the band's use and be told by the driver, 'Mr Womack, you should catch a cab.' I felt like I was being disrespected.

Worse, one time I came out of the studio and was

walking up 49th Street when a couple of gorillas began following me. Walking behind me, real slow, like they were weighing up a mark to roll. I was so fucking mad at having to walk back to the hotel after a hard day in the studio that I turned and told them straight. I said, 'You motherfuckers, fuck with me now and I will kill you.' Oh, man, I was pissed.

CHAPTER 17

WHERE DO WE GO FROM HERE

After about 18 years of marriage, Regina wanted to try and find herself. Come the start of the 1990s, she went to live in New York and took our daughter Ginaree with her.

I have figured all the reasons why she up and left.

A friend said it was because I got abusive. I used to get mad because she would stay out all night. I said, 'I been there and done that. Don't call me at five, saying you're at some club or some house, hanging out, drinking or whatever. I don't feel like I'm married.'

I tried to put fear in her. I said, 'Every time you come home at four or five in the morning I'm going to jump on you.' But it didn't work. Regina left. I got used to people walking in and out of my life.

The first Caucasian girl I went with was Jody Laba. I never had an interest in being with a white woman, or even thought about it, really, probably because of all the problems that I saw as a kid when I was growing up.

Like the case of Emmett Till. Till, from Chicago, went down to Mississippi in 1955 and whistled at a white lady. That earned him a death sentence. The rednecks beat him to a pulp. Cut off his tongue. Cut off his balls. Knocked his right eye out of its socket, his left eye into oblivion. Knocked out most of his teeth. Cut off an ear and took an axe to what remained of his head.

His mother insisted he was left untouched, face up, in an open casket at the funeral. He didn't know he wasn't supposed to wolf whistle.

My father used to say that's why white folks hang us, 'cos they think black men want their women. We would go down South as kids and stay with relatives. We were cocky, but when we went South Dad always said, 'I don't want you all to make any ruckus. From here on in, it is "yes, sir, no, sir".' He wanted us scared.

Till going down to Money, Mississippi, and not coming back, that kind of thing did scare me. His death had a profound effect on me. A lot more things could have been changed if there had been more Sam Cookes or Martin Luther Kings ready to step up.

So, I was taught to stay clear of white folk. My dad didn't invent racism, but he ran his own school. He said, 'Boy, get away from them. Get with your own.' He also argued that the white man had made Jesus white, but there was no proof that he was. 'How do you know? Do you think they had a camera back then?'

I couldn't laugh at things like that or he'd get mad and reach for the strap. My mindset was fixed. I didn't want anybody chasing me, giving me the evil eye or trying to hurt my family because I was hooked up with a white woman. How could I fall in love with a woman that was white? That was the attitude. The whole thing had diseased my mind.

So I always stayed away from it. Honestly? I always felt more comfortable walking into a gig with a black woman on my arm than I ever would if she was white. I knew people would make a fuss over it, same way I got ostracised after marrying Barbara. Life was tough enough without adding to the problems so I had just figured it out of my mind.

Then, in 1994, I walked into Jerry's, a deli on Beverly Boulevard in Los Angeles, and saw Jody. She was working there at the time. Jody was Swedish, from Chicago. It was a strange thing with Jody. I would keep going back to that deli and flirt with her. I thought she was very pretty.

I got sick of corned beef, though. I bought so many corned beef sandwiches to keep the management happy that I had to keep stuffing them in my pocket and tossing them in the trash when I got outside.

Me and Jody, we'd laugh and joke about stuff, things like me putting her in one of my music videos. Never happened and I was always promising it. I guessed she was Swedish, told her I travelled the world and had met a bunch of Swedes. I hadn't. One thing I knew was that in Europe the race issue wasn't like America. One lady over there named her baby after me. He was white. It wasn't an issue.

'You want a corned beef?

'I'm tired of those. I jus' come up here to talk to you.'

The talking didn't go anywhere serious. After a few weeks of this, I turned up at home and there was Jody with a guy in a garage by the apartment block. A big coincidence.

'Didn't know you lived here.'

'Me neither.'

'See you around.'

And I did, by the pool. Now, I never used the pool in this complex. However, I knew Jody loved sunbathing and swimming so I sneaked up to have a look, catch Jody without her clothes on. She looked fine in her itty bitty bikini.

I was still working out my feelings, though. All the things I had run from in my life, knowing the problems caused – or I thought had been caused – because of some blonde-haired, blue-eyed princess. I had become arrogant, had copped a fuck 'em attitude. Fuck women. I shouldn't give her the satisfaction that I was interested.

But I was. I asked if she sang. She did. I asked her out for dinner. We went to Martonis, the last place Sam Cooke visited before he was killed.

First off, I was worried about who might be looking at me in a restaurant with a white girl. We got talking, not flirting this time. I asked her what brought her from Chicago out to California. It was tragic. Her father had been a musician, but hadn't made it and committed suicide. Right after that, her brother had fallen asleep at the wheel of his car and crashed. Killed. He was on his way to becoming a pro jock.

Because my son, Vincent, had committed suicide, we had an immediate connection and that's what we talked about mostly that first night. I forgot about who might be watching a black man with a white girl out on a date. Didn't care.

Jody told me she had run away, couldn't face talking to anybody about it or watching her family suffer. I did all of that, and so I cried. Barbara had always insisted that I should never talk about Vincent. Not to bring it up, ever. That's how she wanted to keep his name. I thought it might help others cope, but she wasn't into saving. Told me just don't mention it.

So no one had really asked me about my son or how he had committed suicide. It was like they wanted to give me that space and not pressure me. I probably didn't know what to say anyway.

But that's when I opened up to her, Jody and I talked it out and we hit it off real close. We had that tragedy in common, and because she was so straight I wanted to keep her around. Also, I noticed, her eyes were clear blue.

Problem was, she had a boyfriend – the guy I saw her with in the garage that time. Actually, he was her fiancé. I was recording an album, *Resurrection*, for the Continuum label. Jody could sing so I took her down to the studio while I cut the album and had her doing vocals with me. It was everything I wanted to say right then,

261

which was I'd come back to life again. Resurrection. With a white girl.

But when I called her apartment, the fiancé would pick up. He'd tell me she was asleep, morning, noon and night. Every time I called up, same story: 'She's sleeping.' I went by Jody's place and eventually got hold of her, told her I'd been trying to reach her and her man said she was asleep. Jody never got any of those messages.

Despite this, we got close. We would go out driving in her car and I would try to touch her fingers, just her little pinkie. Brush it. She would tell me off. 'I'm really engaged to be married,' she insisted.

I played around with that. 'Wow, that's really beautiful, maybe you'll let me sing at the wedding.'

It got where the fiancé began to resent our relationship. I started calling him The Weasel. He looked like one too. He told me one time that he didn't want his girl messed up in – or by – the music business. By then, I was paying her $2000 a day to help me with vocals.

The Weasel said music was all Jody had ever wanted to do. He told me one time, 'I made a commitment to her that, if anybody came in and was serious and wanted to do something for her like you're doing, I would fully support it, but I didn't think it would happen. I didn't think no one would come in.' Then he asked me to lie. 'I want you to do me a favour: please tell Jody she can't sing.' She can't sing? She was all over my album at that point, but he kept on at me. Begged me, 'Tell her she can't sing. You got to do this.'

Then he called Jody's mom and told her his fiancée was running with an 'old nigger'. He reckoned if she was going to run out on him the least she could do was run around with a young one.

That all got back to Jody. They had a row. It ended when he put all her stuff out in the hall, outside my apartment. It was all there, Jody's clothes, make-up, books, pictures, records, the lot, when we got back from the studio one time around four in the morning.

Oh, man. It was my fault, I felt responsible, so I told her to stay a few nights, until she got herself together: on the couch. Yeah, she thought the couch would do it. She ended up staying a while, but then the fiancé decided he wanted her back. He came around at all times banging his fist on my front door, calling her name. I couldn't sleep. I had to get my old peashooter out, slipped it under my pillow in case he came back with a can of kerosene and wanted to burn us out.

If he wasn't problem enough, I found out some of Jody's family had a problem with our relationship, too. Some of it I was sure was the prejudiced kind of problem. The Weasel was back there feeding them all kinds of stuff about me and they got on the phone to chew me out.

My attitude was I didn't want to sit there and explain. She loved me and I loved her.

Of course, some of my fans were not convinced either. At one gig in Philadelphia, the black women in the audience went crazy as soon as they saw I was with Jody with her blonde hair. One lady ran up behind us and I

263

heard, 'What has happened to you, Bobby?' This was a new experience for me. 'All our brothers, every time they make a bit of money, the first thing they get is a white woman. I never thought I'd see the day.'

Some people checked this scene out and laughed. I said, 'Hey, stay out of my business.' Jody had a stand-up row with the woman and, when we got backstage, I said, 'That's the kind of shit I'm talking about. I want to be fighting racism, but I never thought I'd be fighting it from my side.'

I became angry with all the opposition to us. It looked like we were back to the old days. I didn't want to marry a white chick to go through all the old prejudices. I wouldn't be free because even though I loved her I wouldn't be able to be with her without thinking about people looking at us strange when we walked in places. I didn't think I had to go around and prove myself again.

Jody got pregnant and went back to Chicago to have the baby, and along came a boy. We called him Cory and he was the sweetest-looking kid, one eye blue, like Jody, and one brown, from me. I thought, 'Damn, you're going to fuck yourself up just to make each one of us happy.' But he looked like me, acted like me.

My other son, Bobby, was in jail, so it was great to have another son around, but I started thinking of the problems again of bringing a son up to go through the same shit I went through. Actually, I thought it would be worse for him because he wouldn't know if he was black or white.

What brought me out of that was Jody's sister's kids. They didn't see colours. That taught me a lot. It was me going around fucked up, thinking about black and white hate. People put the hate in children later, taught them about prejudice. Kids don't think like that.

The family finally took me in. They loved Jody and I guess they figured if Jody liked me that much then they had to accept me, but it was still difficult. For Cory's first birthday, I was the only black in the room. Jody was busy waiting on everyone and I felt uneasy sat there. Then my son came over and slept on my lap and I felt like it didn't matter.

We still had our moments, but they were mainly my problems. When Jody mentioned Martin Luther King, I told her to can it. Told her she didn't know what she was talking about. She asked, 'Where do you get off being so defensive, Bobby?'

'Don't mess with Mr King.'

'Why not? I read books.' She couldn't understand why I was so defensive.

I made out I used to hang out with the guy, shoot crap with him, all kinds of shit. Told Jody, 'You know nothing about Martin Luther King so don't start making out you know how black people feel.'

Jody was mad. 'You are ridiculous.'

That was kind of an epiphany. Yeah, what was the problem? Stuff was said on TV, racial things I heard in the street, but it wasn't everyone. It wasn't Jody. I couldn't blame everyone.

We weathered that and a lot of other shit besides. What we couldn't weather was the Los Angeles earthquake in 1994. The big one. I lived over the hills in Sherman Oaks at that time, with Jody.

First thing I thought was I'd had some bad cocaine. When the shaking started, I said, 'Oh, Lord, if you ever let me get out I'll never do it again.' I got down on the floor, lay by the bed and prayed. Prayed like crazy. I mean *really* prayed.

Jody rushed in to find me and I told her, 'I have sinned so much, it's not you, it's me he wants.'

All my stuff in the apartment was toppled over and crashed about the place. I had two statues from Africa in the bedroom and the fuckers jumped up and down with all the shaking. They looked like they had come alive. I asked Jody to lie on top of me.

'Why on top of you?'

''Cos that's what you do when something like this happens, it's the way to protect each other.'

She wasn't convinced. 'And, while I lie on top, the TV falls on my head.'

It felt like that earthquake lasted hours, but was probably only minutes. I couldn't see anything in the halls, the elevators were out and people were running down the stairs. The whole apartment block was swaying, rattling and rolling. Outside was like a war zone and the LA residents had become refugees in it, walking around in their pyjamas.

The end game was Jody went back to Chicago. She

didn't want to stay in LA if there was another chance of an earthquake. I guess the earthquake must have been stronger than our love, but we're still very close.

We had another boy after – Jordan. It bothers me I'm not able to see the kids as much as I would like, but I have to work weekends. Sometimes both the boys ask why we don't get married, but I think part of it was I just wasn't ready to have a new family simply because I was still attached to Regina, still married to her.

I've gotten ready to be a senior citizen. I'm holed up in Sherman Oaks, Los Angeles. Been in the same apartment I've been in for more than a decade. It's OK. I go out nights, ride my bike or run, and no one bothers me. I haven't done drugs in a long, long time. The wine in the rack has been there four years or more. Haven't touched a drop of it.

Alone now and I take it one day at a time. Go to bed, fall asleep at four, come awake at eight or nine. I feel like I'm adjusting like a person who has been in a wheelchair and taking their first steps. My main thing now is to do the gig and leave.

It's sad. I don't speak to Barbara no more; Linda doesn't speak to her. Haven't spoken to Cecil for years. No one speaks to no one.

Don't know where Sly is at. I hear all kinds of stories, but I love him. If he made the turn I made, then we could talk. That would be beautiful, but it is what it is and life goes on.

Pickett I hadn't heard from for a while by the time he died. I don't talk to Jim Ford, but think about him all the time. And sometimes, when you don't hear anything, then you assume people are doing OK, and that is better than if they called and they are not doing so good.

I don't even try to talk to women now. Don't need one. I ran out of energy. I don't pick them up or see anyone else, not with this ton of baggage I still got. I guess I could tell them I got two kids in Chicago, one in New York, another in jail and two deceased. That's enough.

CHRONOLOGY

1930s
Five Blind Boys of Mississippi form at Piney Woods
School near Jackson, Mississippi

22 January 1931
Sam Cooke born Clarksdale, Mississippi

18 March 1941
Wilson Pickett born Prattville, Alabama

4 March 1944
Bobby Dwayne Womack born Cleveland, Ohio

15 March 1944
Sly Stone (Sylvester Stewart) born Denton, Texas

1951
Pop Staples forms the Staples Singers

1953
Bobby meets Sam Cooke when the Womack Brothers
opens for Cooke's band The Soul Stirrers

1954
Bobby makes his debut in a studio when the
Womack Brothers make their first record

August 1955
Black teenager Emmett Till is murdered for allegedly
whistling at a white woman in Mississippi

December
Rosa Parks refuses to give up her seat on a bus to a white
passenger, triggering a boycott of the local bus system

1957
Sam Cooke quits The Soul Stirrers

1961
Sam Cooke sets up SAR Records in Los Angeles
and signs The Womack Brothers, who later become
The Valentinos
Marvin Gaye is signed to Motown

July 1962
The Valentinos score first hit with 'Lookin' For A Love'

July 1963
Sam Cooke's son Vincent drowns in the swimming pool
of the house on Ames Street, Los Feliz, Los Angeles.

August
Martin Luther King delivers his 'I have a dream'
speech in Washington

November
President John F Kennedy assassinated in Dallas, Texas

June 1964
The Rolling Stones score first UK No 1 with
a cover of Bobby's 'It's All Over Now'
August 'It's All Over Now' is not a hit for
The Valentinos

11 December 1964
Sam Cooke shot dead by Bertha Franklin in a
Los Angeles motel

March 1965 Bobby marries Barbara Cooke

August 1965 'In The Midnight Hour' is an R&B hit
for Wilson Pickett
The Voting Rights Act is passed in a bid to make the
voting system fairer for black Americans

1967 Sly and the Family Stone form in San Francisco

September 1967
'Trust Me' is first solo release by Bobby

December
Otis Redding dies in a plane crash at the age of 26

1968
Bobby and Wilson Pickett team up. Pickett has a
hit with Bobby's 'Midnight Mover'

1970
Bobby and Barbara divorce
May Marvin Gaye releases *What's Going On*

September 1970
Jimi Hendrix dies

October 1970
Janis Joplin dies

November 1971
Bobby plays guitar on Sly And The Family Stone's
There's A Riot Going On

1974
Bobby's brother Harry is stabbed to death
Bobby meets Ronnie Wood and joins The Faces
on their last tour

1976
Bobby meets and in December marries Regina Banks

1978
Death of Bobby's infant son, Truth Bobby

1980
Bobby signs to Beverley Glen

1981
Friendly Womack, Bobby's father, dies

October 1982
Marvin Gaye releases 'Sexual Healing'

April 1984
Marvin Gaye shot dead by his father Marvin Sr

1986

Rolling Stones use Bobby on the album *Dirty Work* and and sings vocals on 'Harlem Shuffle'

1993

Bobby meets Jody Laba. The couple have two boys, Cory and Jordan

1997

Quentin Tarantino reprises Bobby's 1973 hit 'Across 110th Street' for title theme to his movie *Jackie Brown*, starring Bobby's former girlfriend Pam Grier

January 2001

Bobby contributes 'I'm Your Puppet' to *Meet The Parents* soundtrack

DISCOGRAPHY

n/i – not issued
n/e – no chart entry

TITLE	LABEL	UK	US
THE WOMACK BROTHERS			
SINGLES			
1961			
Somebody's Wrong/Yield Not To Temptation	SAR	n/i	n/e
[Other unreleased tracks recorded as			
The Womack Brothers include			
'Couldn't Hear Nobody Pray' and			
'Somewhere There's A God', later changed			
to 'Somewhere There's A Girl']			
THE VALENTINOS			
SINGLES			
July 1962			
Lookin' For A Love/Somewhere			
There's A Girl	SAR	n/i	72
September 1962			
I'll Make It Alright/Darling Come Back Home	SAR	n/i	97

TITLE	LABEL	UK	US
1962			
She's So Good To Me/Baby Lots Of Luck	SAR	n/i	n/e
June 1964			
It's All Over Now/Tired Of Living			
In The Country	SAR	n/i	94
September 1964			
Everyone Wants To Fall In Love/			
Bitter Dreams	SAR	n/i	n/e
[Bobby split from The Valentinos in 1964.			
Several further singles were issued by			
the remaining brothers]			
1966			
What About Me	Chess	n/i	n/e
October 1966			
Sweeter Than The Day Before	Chess	n/i	n/e
1968			
It's All Over Now/			
Tired Of Living In The Country	Soul City	n/e	n/i
[Unreleased tracks by The Valentinos include			
'I've Got A Girl' and 'I've Got Love For You']			

ALBUM
1968

Double Barrelled Soul	Soul City	n/e	n/e

TITLE	LABEL	UK	US

BOBBY WOMACK

SINGLES

1965
I Found A True Love/A Lonesome Man — Chess — n/i — n/e

1965
Nothing You Can Do — Him — n/i — n/e

September 1967
Trust Me/Baby I Can't Stand It — Minit — n/i — n/e

February 1968
Broadway Walk/Somebody Special — Minit — n/e — n/e

April 1968
What Is This/What You Gonna Do
(WhenYour Love Has Gone) — Minit — n/e — n/e

August 1968
Fly Me To The Moon/Take Me — Minit — n/e — 52

December 1968
Californian Dreamin'/
Baby You Oughta Think It Over — Minit — n/e — 43

April 1969
I Left My Heart In San Francisco/
Love, The Time Is Now — Minit — n/i — n/e

July 1969
It's Gonna Rain/Thank You — Minit — n/i — n/e

TITLE	LABEL	UK	US
November 1969			
How I Miss You Baby/Tired And Convicted	Minit	n/i	93
April 1970			
More Than I Can Stand/Arkansas State Prison	Minit	n/i	90
June 1970			
I'm Gonna Forget About You/Don't Look Back	Liberty	n/i	n/e
December 1970			
Something/Everybody's Talkin'	Liberty	n/i	n/e
December 1971			
That's The Way I Feel About Cha/ Come L'Amore	United Artists	n/e	27
May 1972			
Woman's Gotta Have It/ If You Don't Want My Love	United Artists	n/e	60
August 1972			
Sweet Caroline/Harry Hippie	United Artists	n/e	51
December 1972			
Harry Hippie/I can Understand It	United Artists	n/e	31
January 1973			
Across 110th Street/Hang On In There	United Artists	n/e	56
June 1973			
Nobody Wants You When You're Down And Out/ I'm Through Trying To Prove My Love For You	United Artists	n/e	29

DISCOGRAPHY

TITLE	LABEL	UK	US
February 1974			
Lookin' For A Love/			
Let It All Hang Out	United Artists	n/e	10
June 1974			
You're Welcome, Stop On By	United Artists	n/i	59
April 1975			
Check It Out/Interlude No 2	United Artists	n/e	91
November 1975			
Where There's A Will There's A Way/			
Everything's Gonna Be Alright	United Artists	n/e	n/e
March 1976			
Daylight/Trust Me	United Artists	n/e	n/e
October 1976			
Home Is Where The Heart Is/			
We've Only Just Begun	CBS/Columbia	n/e	n/e
1978			
Wind It Up/Stop Before We Start	CBS/Columbia	n/i	n/e
June 1979			
I Honestly Love You/			
How Could You Break My Heart	Arista	n/i	n/e
August 1979			
Roads Of Life/Give It Up	Arista	n/i	n/e

TITLE	LABEL	UK	US
February 1982			
Secrets/Stand Up	Motown/		
	Beverly Glen	n/e	n/e
July 1982			
So Many Sides Of You/	Motown/		
Just My Imagination	Beverly Glen	n/e	n/i
March 1984			
Love Has Finally Come	Motown/		
(with Patti Labelle)/	Beverly Glen)	n/i	88
American Dream			
June 1984			
Tell Me Why/	Motown	60	n/e
Through The Eyes Of A Child			
September 1984			
Surprise Surprise/American Dream	Beverly Glen	n/e	n/e
September 1984			
It Takes A Lot Of Strength To Say Goodbye	Beverly Glen	n/i	n/e
(with Patti Labelle)/Who's Foolin' Who			
January 1985			
I Wish I Had Someone To Go Home To/	Beverly Glen	n/i	n/e
Someday We'll All Be Free			
March 1985			
Searching For My Love/I'm So Proud	Beverly Glen	n/i	n/e

TITLE	LABEL	UK	US
September 1985			
I Wish He Didn't Trust Me So Much/	MCA	64	n/e
Got To Be With You Tonight			
May 1986			
Gypsy Woman/			
Whatever Happened To The Times	MCA	n/e	n/e
January 1987			
I Wanna Make Love To You/	MCA	n/e	n/e
Whatever Happened To The Times			
October 1987			
Living In A Box	MCA	70	n/e
August 1994			
Forever Love/Colour Him Father	Continuum	n/e	n/e
June 2004			
Califonia Dreamin'	EMI	59	n/e

ALBUMS

August 1968			
Fly Me To The Moon	Minit	n/i	n/e
Fly Me To The Moon • Baby!			
You Oughta Think It Over			
I'm A Midnight Mover • What Is This			
Somebody Special • Take Me			
Moonlight In Vermont			

TITLE	LABEL	UK	US

Love, The Time Is Now • I'm In Love
California Dreamin' • No Money In My Pocket
Lillie Mae

1969

My Prescription   Minit
How I Miss You Baby • More Than I Can Stand
It's Gonna Rain • Everyone's Gone To The Moon
I Can't Take It Like A Man •
I Left My Heart In San Francisco •
Arkansas State Prison •
I'm Gonna Forget About You • Don't Look Back
Tried And Convicted • Thank You

1970

The Womack Live (Live '68)   Liberty   n/i   n/e
Let It Out • Intro • Oh How I Miss You Baby
California Dreamin' • Something
Everybody's Talkin' •
Medley: Laughing And Clowning,
To Live The Past, I'm A Midnight Mover,
The Preacher, More Than I Can Stand

December 1971

Communication   United Artists n/e   83
Communication • Come l'Amore
Fire and Rain • (If You Don't Want My Love)
Give It Back • Medley: Monologue/
They Long to Be, Close to You
Everything Is Beautiful
That's the Way I Feel About 'Cha
Yield Not to Temptation

TITLE	LABEL	UK	US

June 1972

Understanding   United Artists   n/e   43

I Can Understand It • Woman's Gotta Have It
And I Love Her • Got To Get You Back
Simple Man • Ruby Dean • Thing Called Love
Sweet Caroline • Harry Hippie

January 1973

Across 110th Street   United Artists   n/e   50

Across 110th Street • We Thought We Were OK
Harlem Clavinette • If You Don't Want My Love
Punk Errand Boy • Hang on in There • Man
Quicksand • 150 Rounds • Harlem Love Theme
Sick And Tired • Across 110th Street
Take the Money • Do It Right • Hang on in There
If You Don't Want My Love • This Is the Police
Across 110th Street

July 1973

Facts Of Life   United Artists   n/e   37

Nobody Wants You When You're Down and Out
I'm Through Trying to Prove My Love to You
If You Can't Give Her Love, Give Her Up
That's Heaven to Me
Medley: Holdin' On To My Baby's Love/Nobody
Medley: Fact of Life/
He'll Be There When The Sun Goes Down
Can't Stop Man In Love • Look Of Love
Natural Man • All Along The Watchtower

TITLE	LABEL	UK	US
December 1973			
Lookin' For A Love Again	United Artists	n/e	85
Looking For A Love			
I Don't Wanna Be Hurt By Ya Love Again			
Doing It My Way • Let It Hang Out			
Point Of No Return			
You're Welcome, Stop On By			
You're Messing Up A Good Thing			
Don't Let Me Down • Copper Kettle			
There's One Thing That Beats Falling			
May 1975			
I Don't Know What The World Is Coming To	United Artists	n/e	n/e
Interlude #1/ I Don't Know • Superstar			
(If You Want My Love) Put Something Down On It			
Git It • What's Your World • Check It Out			
Interlude #2 • Jealous Love • It's All Over Now			
Yes, Jesus Loves Me			
December 1975			
Safety Zone	United Artists	n/e	n/e
Everythin's Gonna Be Allright			
I Wish It Would Rain • Trust In Me			
Where There's A Will, There's A Way			
Love Ain't Something You Can Get For Free			
Something You Got • Daylight			
I Feel A Groove Coming On			
April 1976			
BW Goes C&W	United Artists	n/e	n/e
Don't Make This Last Date For You And Me			
Behind Closed Doors • Bouquet Roses			

TITLE	LABEL	UK	US
Tired Of Living In The Country • Tarnished Rings			
Big Bayou • Song Of The Mockingbird			
I'd Be Ahead If I Could Quit While I'm Behind			
You • I Take It Home			

September 1976

Home Is Where The Heart Is	Columbia	n/e	n/e

Home Is Where The Heart Is • A Little Bit Salty
Standing In The Safety Zone
One More Chance On Love
How Long (Has This Been Going On)
I Could Never Be Satisfied
Something For My Head
A Change Is Gonna Come
We've Only Just Begun

July 1978

Pieces	Liberty	n/i	n/e

It's Party Time • Trust Your Heart
Stop Before We Start
When Love Begins Friendship Ends
Wind It Up • Is This The Thanks I Get
Caught Up In The Middle
Never Let Nothing Get The Best Of You

July 1979

Roads Of Life	Arista	n/e	n/e

Roads of Life • How Could You Break My Heart
Honey Dripper Boogie • Roots in Me
What Are You Doin' • Give It Up
Mr DJ Don't Stop the Music
I Honestly Love You

MIDNIGHT MOVER

TITLE	LABEL	UK	US

1979

Save The Children — Solar — n/e n/e
Save The Children • Priorities
Too Close For Comfort • Baby I'm Back
She's My Girl • Free Love • How Can It Be
Tough Job • Now We're Together • Better Love

January 1982

The Poet — Beverly Glen — n/e 29
So Many Sides Of You • Lay Your Lovin' On Me
Secrets • Just My Imagination • Stand Up
Games • If You Think You're Lonely Now
Where Do We Go From Here

March 1984

The Poet II — Motown/ — 31 60
Love Has Finally Come at Last — Beverly Glen
It Takes a Lot of Strength to Say Goodbye
Through the Eyes of a Child • Surprise, Surprise
Tryin' To Get over You • Tell Me Why
Who's Foolin' Who
I Wish I Had Someone to Go Home To
American Dream

August 1985

So Many Rivers — MCA — n/e 66
I Wish He Didn't Trust Me So Much
So Baby, Don't Leave Home Without It
So Many Rivers • Got To Be With You Tonight
Gypsy Woman
Whatever Happened To The Times?
Let Me Kiss It Where It Hurts • Only Survivor
That's Where It's At • Check It Out

TITLE	LABEL	UK	US
July 1986			
Womagic	MCA	n/e	n/e
I Wanna Make Love To You			
When The Weekend Comes			
All The Things You Do			
I Can't Stay Mad Too Long			
Hear The Music • Outside Myself			
I Ain't Got To Live Nobody Else			
More Than Love • It Ain't Me			
November 1987			
The Last Soul Man	MCA	n/e	n/e
Living In A Box • When The Weekend Comes			
Still Love You • Gina			
A World Where No One Cries			
A Woman Likes To Hear That			
Real Love Please Stand Up			
The things We Do (When We're Lonely)			
Falling In Love Again • Outside Myself			
1994			
Resurrection	Continuum	n/e	n/e
Good Ole Days • You Made Me Love Again			
So High On Your Love			
Don't Break Your Promise (Too Soon)			
Forever Love • Please Change Your Mind			
Trying Not To Break Down • Cousin Henry			
Centerfield • Goin' Home			
Walkin On The Wildside • Cry Myself To Sleep			
Wish • Color Him Father			

TITLE	LABEL	UK	US

1999

Back To My Roots unknown unknown

Opening Narration • Rug • Stand by Me

Oh Happy Day • Jesus Be a Fence Around Me

What a Friend We Have in Jesus

Where There's A Will There's A Way

I'm Coming Home • It Is Well • Motherless Child

Bridge over Troubled Water • Looking Back

Ease My Troubled Mind

Nearer My God to Thee • Cousin Henry

Hundred Pounds of Clay

Amen/This Little Light of Mine/Closing Narration

1999

Traditions Capitol n/e n/e

Dear Santa Claus • This Christmas

Have Yourself a Merry Little Christmas

Christmas Ain't Christmas • White Christmas

First Noel • Hark! The Herald Angels Sing

Christmas Song • Silent Night • Jingle Bells

Dear Santa Claus • Winter Wonderland

O Holy Night • Rudolph the Red-Nosed Reindeer

Away in a Manger • Joy to the World

Auld Lang Syne

OTHER RECORDINGS

Before and during his solo career Bobby Womack also had a hand in many records by other artists either as writer (w), a featured vocalist(s), a session musician/guitarist(m) or a combination of those.

TITLE	LABEL	UK	US

SAM COOKE

SINGLES

February 1962

Twistin' The Night Away(m)/One More Time   RCA   6   9

June 1962

Having A Party(m)/Bring It On Home To Me (m)   RCA   n/e 17

October1962

Nothing Can Change This Love(m)/

Somebody Have Mercy (m)   RCA   n/e 12

January 1963

Send Me Some Loving(m)/Baby Baby Baby(m) RCA   n/e 13

April 1963

Another Saturday Night(m)/

Love Will Find A Way   RCA   23 10

August 1963

Frankie And Johnny(m)/Cool Train   RCA   30 11

October 1963

Little Red Rooster(m)/You've Gotta Move   RCA   n/i 11

February 1964

(Ain't That) Good News(m)/Basin Street Blues RCA   n/e 11

June 1964

Good Times(m)/Tennessee Waltz (m)   RCA   n/e 11

TITLE	LABEL	UK	US
October 1964			
Cousin Of Mine(m)/That's Where It Is At (m)	RCA	n/e	31
January 1965			
Shake(m)/A Change Is Gonna Come (m)	RCA	n/e	7
March 1965			
It's Got The Whole World Shakin'(m)/			
Ease My Troubled Mind	RCA	n/e	41
June 1965			
When A Boy Falls In Love(m)/The Piper	RCA	n/e	52
August 1965			
Sugar Dumpling(m)/Bridge Of Tears	RCA	n/e	32
January1966			
Feel It (m)/That's All	RCA	n/e	95

ALBUMS

May 1962
Twistin' the Night Away RCA n/e 72
Twistin' The Night Away • Sugar Dumpling
Twistin' In The Kitchen With Dinah
Somebody's Gonna Miss Me
A whole Lotta Woman • The Twist
Twistin' In The Old Town Tonight
Movin' And A-Groovin' • Clamptown Twist
Somebody Have Mercy • Soothe Me
That's It I Quit – I'm Movin' On

TITLE	LABEL	UK	US
March 1963			
Mr Soul	RCA	n/e	94

I Wish You Love • Willow Weep For Me
Chains Of Love • Smoke Rings • All The Way
Send Me Some Lovin' • Cry Me A River
Driftin' Blues •
(I Love You For) Sentimental Reasons
Nothing Can Change This Love • Little Girl
These Foolish Things

TITLE	LABEL	UK	US
September 1963			
Night Beat	RCA	n/i	62

Nobody Knows The Trouble I've Seen
Lost And Lookin' • Mean Old World
Please Don't Drive Me Away • I Lost Everything
Get Yourself Another Fool • Little Red Rooster
Laughin' And Clowin' • Trouble Blues
You Gotta Move • Fool's Paradise
Shake Rattle And Roll

TITLE	LABEL	UK	US
March 1964			
Ain't That Good News	RCA	n/e	34

Ain't That Good News
Meet Me At Mary's Place • Good Times
Rome Wasn't Built In A Day
Another Saturday Night • Tennessee Waltz
Falling In Love • Home • Sittin' In the Sun
No Second Time • The Riddle Song

TITLE	LABEL	UK	US
February 1965			
Shake	RCA	n/e	44

Shake • Yeah Man • Win Your Love For Me

Lover You Most Of All • Meet Me At Mary's Place

I've Got The Whole World Shakin'

A Change Is Gonna Come

I'm In The Mood For Love

I'm Just A Country Boy

You're Nobody 'Til Somebody Loves You

 Comes Love • Ease My Troublin' Mind

THE BOX TOPS

SINGLES

TITLE	LABEL	UK	US
July 1967			
The Letter (m)/Happy Times	Stateside/Mala	5	1
November 1967			
Neon Rainbow (m)/She Knows How	Stateside/Mala	n/e	24

WILSON PICKETT

SINGLES

TITLE	LABEL	UK	US
October 1967			
I'm In Love (w/m)	Atlantic	n/i	45
February 1968			
Jealous Love(m)/I've Come A Long Way (m)	Atlantic	n/i	50
April 1968			
She's Looking Good(m)/We've Got To Have Love	Atlantic	n/e	15

TITLE	LABEL	UK	US
June 1968			
I'm A Midnight Mover (w/m)/Deborah	Atlantic	38	24
September 1968			
I Found A True Love (w/m)/For Better Or Worse	Atlantic	n/e	42
November 1968			
A Man And A Half (w/m)/			
People Make The World (What It Is)	Atlantic	n/i	42
December 1968			
Hey Jude (m)/Night Owl	Atlantic	16	n/i
March 1969			
Mini Skirt Minnie (m)/Back In Your Arms	Atlantic	n/e	50
March 1969			
Born To Be Wild (m)/Toe Hold	Atlantic	n/i	64
July 1969			
Hey Joe (m)/Night Owl	Atlantic	n/i	59
November 1969			
You Keep Me Hanging On (m)/			
Now You See Me, Now You Don't	Atlantic	n/e	92
May 1970			
Sugar Sugar/Cole, Cooke and Redding (w/m)	Atlantic	n/e	25

ALBUMS

February 1968			
I'm In Love	Atlantic	n/e	70

TITLE	LABEL	UK	US
Jealous Love • Stagger Lee • That Kind Of Love			
I'm In Love • Hello Sunshine			
Don't Cry No More			
We've Got To Have Love			
Bring it On Home To Me • She's Looking Good			
I've Come A Long Way			

July 1969

The Midnight Mover	Atlantic	n/e	91

I'm A Midnight Mover • It's A Groove
Remember I Been Good To You • I'm Gonna Cry
Deborah • I Found A True Love
Down By The Sea • Trust Me
Let's Get An Understanding
For Better Or Worse

ROLLING STONES
SINGLES
August 1964

It's All Over Now (w)/Good Times Bad Times	Decca/London	1	26

March 1986

Harlem Shuffle (s)/Had It With You	CBS/Columbia	13	5

ALBUM
March 1986

Dirty Work (s)	CBS/Columbia	4	4

One Hit To The Body • Fight • Harlem Shuffle
Hold Back • Too Rude • Winning Ugly
Back To Zero • Dirty Work • Had It With You
Sleep Tonight

TITLE	LABEL	UK	US

ELVIS PRESLEY
SINGLES

September 1969

Suspicious Minds (m)/	RCA	2	1

You'll Think Of Me

JANIS JOPLIN
SINGLES

May 1971

Cry Baby/Mercedes Benz (m)	CBS/Columbia	n/e	42

ALBUM

January 1971

Pearl	CBS/Columbia	50	1

Move Over • Cry Baby • A Woman Left Lonely
Half Moon • Buried Alive In the Blues
My Baby • Me and Bobby McGee
Mercedes Benz • Trust Me(w • m)
Get It While You Can

SLY AND THE FAMILY STONE
SINGLES

October 1971

Family Affair(m)/Luv 'n' Haight	Epic	15	1

ALBUM

November 1971

There's A Riot Going On (m)	Epic	31	1

Luv'n' Haight • Just Like A Baby • Poet
Family Affair • Africa Talks To You

TITLE	LABEL	UK	US
The Asphalt Jungle • Brave & Strong			
(You Caught Me) Smilin' • Time			
Spaced Cowboy • Runnin' Away			
Thank You For Talkin' To Me Africa			

RAY CHARLES

SINGLES

December 1965

Crying Time (m)/	ABC Paramount/		
When My Dream Boat Comes Home	HMV	n/e	6

April 1966

Together Again (m)/	ABC Paramount/		
Just About To Lose Your Crown (m)	HMV	48	19

June 1966

Let's Go Get Stoned (m)/	ABC Paramount/		
The Train	HMV	n/e	31

September 1966

I Choose To Sing The Blues (m)/Hopelessly	ABC Paramount/		
	HMV	n/e	32

November 1966

Please Say You're Fooling (m)/	ABC Paramount/		
I Don't Need No Doctor (m)	HMV	n/e	64

February 1967

I Want To Talk About You (m)/	ABC Paramount/		
Please Say You're Fooling (m)	HMV	n/e	98

TITLE	LABEL	UK	US
June 1967			
Here We Go Again (m)/	ABC Tangerine/		
Somebody Ought To Write A Book	HMV	38	15
About It			
August 1967			
In The Heat Of The Night (m)/	ABC Tangerine/		
Something's Got To Change	HMV	n/e	33
November 1967			
Yesterday(m)/	ABC Tangerine/		
Never Had Enough Of Nothing Yet	Stateside	44	25
February 1968			
That's A Lie (m)/Go On Home	ABC Tangerine/		
	Stateside	n/e	64
July 1968			
Eleanor Rigby (m)/Understanding (m)	ABC Tangerine/		
	Stateside	36	35

ALBUMS

Crying Time

March 1966	HMV/ABC		
Crying Time • No Use Crying	Paramount	n/e	15

Let's Go Get Stoned • Going Down Slow
Peace Of Mind • Tears • Drifting Blues
We Don't See Eye To Eye
You're In For A Big Surprise
You're Just About To Lose Your Crown
Don't You Think I Ought To Know
You've Got A Problem

TITLE	LABEL	UK	US
September 1966			
Ray's Moods	HMV/ABC		
What'cha Doing In There (I Wanna Know)	Paramount	n /e	52
Please Say You're Fooling			
By The Light Of The Silvery Moon			
You Don't Understand			
Maybe It's Because Of Love			
Chitlins With Candied Yams			
Granny Wasn't Grinning That Day			
She's Lonesome Again • Sentimental Journey			
A Born Loser • It's A Man's World			
A Girl I Used To Know			
July 1967			
Ray Charles Invites You To Listen	HMV/ABC		
She's Funny That Way	Tangerine	n/e	76
(I Got A Woman Crazy For Me)			
How Deep Is The Ocean (How High Is The Sky)			
You Made Me Love You (I Didn't Wanna Do It)			
Yesterday • I'll Be Seeing You			
Here We Go Again • All For You			
Love Walked In • Gee, Baby Ain't I Good To You			
People			
April 1968			
A Portrait Of Ray	HMV/ABC		
Eleanor Rigby • Am I Blue • Never Say Naw	Tangerine	n/e	51
Sun Died • Yesterday • When I Stop Dreaming			
I Won't Leave • Sweet Young Thing Like You			
Bright Lights And You Girl • Understanding			

298

TITLE	LABEL	UK	US
ARETHA FRANKLIN			
SINGLES			
March 1967			
I Never Loved A Man (The Way I Love You) (m)/	Atlantic	n/e	9
Do Right Woman, Do Right Man			
August 1967			
Baby I Love You (m)/Going Down Slow	Atlantic	39	4
October 1967			
(You Make Me Feel Like A) Natural Woman (m)/	Atlantic	n/i	8
Baby Baby Baby			
November 1967			
Chain Of Fools (m)/Prove It	Atlantic	n/i	2
1968			
Since You've Been Gone (m)/Ain't No Way (m)	Atlantic	47	5
May 1968			
Think (m)/You Send Me (m)	Atlantic	26	7
October 1971			
Rock Steady (m)/Oh Me Oh My	Atlantic	n/i	9
July 1974			
I'm In Love (w)/Oh Baby	Atlantic	n/e	19
ALBUMS			
July 1967			
I Never Loved A Man The Way I Love You	Atlantic	36	2
Respect • Drown In My Own Tears			

TITLE	LABEL	UK	US
I Never Loved A Man (The Way I Loved You)			
Soul Serenade • Don't Let Me Lose This Dream			
Baby Baby Baby • Dr Feelgood • Good Times			
Do Right Woman, Do Right Man • Save Me			
A Change Is Gonna Come			
February 1968			
Aretha: Lady Soul	Atlantic	25	2
Chain Of Fools • Money Won't Change You			
People Get Ready • Niki Hoeky			
(You Make Me Feel Like) A Natural Woman			
Since You've Been Gone (Sweet Sweet Baby)			
Good To Me As I Am To You • Come Back Baby			
Groovin' • Ain't No Way			

GEORGE BENSON

SINGLES

April 1976

Breezin'(w)/Lady	Warners	n/e	63

DUSTY SPRINGFIELD

SINGLES

December 1968

Son Of A Preacher Man (m)/

Just A Little Lovin' (Early In The Morning)	Philips	9	10

1969

Don't Forget About Me(m)/Breakfast In Bed (m)	Atlantic	n/e	64

TITLE	LABEL	UK	US
1969			
Willie & Laura Mae Jones (m)/			
That Old Sweet Roll (Hi De Ho)	Atlantic	n/e	78
1969			
I Don't Want To Hear It Anymore/			
Windmills Of Your Mind (m)	Atlantic	n/e	31

ALBUMS

	LABEL	UK	US
1969			
Dusty In Memphis(m)	Atlantic	n/e	99

Just A Little Lovin' • So Much Love

Son Of A Preachr Man

I don't Want To Hear It Anymore

Don't Forget About Me • Breakfast In Bed

Just One Smile • The Windmills Of Your Mind

In the Land Of Make Believe

No Easy way Down • I Can't Make It Alone

WILTON FELDER

SINGLES

	LABEL	UK	US
October 1980			
Inherit The Wind (s)/Until The Morning Comes	MCA	39	n/e
1985			
I'll Still Be Lookin' Up To You (s)/La Luz	MCA	63	n/e

ALBUMS

	LABEL	UK	US
November 1980			
Inherit The Wind	MCA	n/e	n/e

TITLE	LABEL	UK	US
Inherit The Wind • Someday We'll All Be Free			
Until The Morning Comes • Insight • LA Light			
I've Got A Secret I'm Gonna Tell			
February 1985			
Secrets	MCA	77	81
Secrets • (No Matter How High I Get)			
I'll Still Be Lookin' Up To You • La Luz			
The Truth Song • I Found You			

DELANEY/BONNIE

SINGLES

January 1972			
Move 'Em Out (m)/Sing My Way Home	Atlanic/Atco	n/i	59
March 1972			
Where There's A Will There's A Way(m)/	Atlantic/Atco	n/i	99
Lonesome And A Long Way From Home			

LULU

SINGLES

April 1993			
I'm Back For More (s)	Dome	27	n/e
Living In A Box			

SINGLES

September 1987			
So The Story Goes(s)	Chrysalis	34	n/e

TITLE	LABEL	UK	US

SHIRLEY BROWN AND BOBBY WOMACK

SINGLES

November 1989

Ain't Nothing Like	Chrysalis/		
The Lovin' We Got(s)	Cooltempo	n/e	n/e

JEANIE TRACY AND BOBBY WOMACK

SINGLES

May 1995

It's A Man's Man's Man's World	Pulse	73	n/e

GABOR SZABO

SINGLES

1971

Breezin'(w/m)	Blue Thumb	Not Known	

1971

Azure Blue(m)	Blue Thumb	Not Known	

ALBUMS

1971

High Contrast	Blue Thumb	Not Known	

Just A Little Communication • J-K Jive
If You Don't Want My Love • Amazon • Fingers
I Remember When • Azure Blue • Breezin' • Junk